MEMBERS
of the
COMMUNITY

Lee Hamill and Ann Dunlevy

IEP
RESOURCES

Lee Hamill and Ann Dunlevy, Authors
Tom Kinney, Editor
Wanda Little, Graphic Design

An Attainment Company Publication
©2000, 2005 Attainment Company, Inc. All rights reserved.
Printed in the United States of America.

ISBN 1-57861-108-3

IEP

RESOURCES

Attainment Company, Inc.
P.O. Box 930160 • Verona, Wisconsin 53593-0160 USA
Phone: 800-327-4269 • Fax: 800.942.3865
www.AttainmentCompany.com

Introduction

Chapter One – Grocery Shopping

Chapter Two – Community Directions

Chapter Three – Mall

Chapter Four – Media

Chapter Five – Recipe Planning

Chapter Six – Hospital

Appendix

ABOUT THE AUTHORS

Lee Hamill

Lee Hamill is currently an assistant professor in the Special Education Program of the Education Department at Xavier University in Cincinnati.

She earned her bachelor's degree in Special Education and her master's degree in Special Education with an emphasis in Curriculum and Materials, at the University of Cincinnati. She completed her Ph.D. in Curriculum and Instruction in Special Education at Indiana University in 1995. Prior to working on her doctorate, Dr. Hamill taught students with developmental handicaps in the Talawanda City School District in Oxford, Ohio. The materials and classroom procedures described in this book were developed and used during Dr. Hamill's tenure in classrooms for students with developmental handicaps. Dr. Hamill has taught both primary and high school students with developmental handicaps and has served as a small-group instructor of ESL students and for students with developmental handicaps in the Talawanda schools. She has also taught fifth grade in a public school and several subject areas in a private, nongraded, open-classroom elementary school in central Maine.

Ann Dunlevy

Ann Dunlevy earned her B.A. at Middlebury College, her M.A. at Northwestern University, and completed two years of post-master's work at Auburn University. She is currently a counselor at the Student Counseling Service, Miami University, Oxford, Ohio. She has worked previously as a high school English teacher, a teacher of gifted children, a high school counselor, a school social worker, and a rehabilitation counselor and administrator. As a school counselor and social worker, Mrs. Dunlevy worked with students with developmental handicaps and their families. For sixteen months she served as a counselor for students and young adults with developmental handicaps in four communities, a program operated jointly by the Maine Division of Vocational Rehabilitation and the Waterville, Maine, school district.

PHOTOCOPY RIGHTS & CD-ROM FILES

Photocopy Rights

IEP Resources grants photocopy rights for personal or educational uses. Teachers may copy pages and distribute them to students for home or school use.

CD-ROM Files

A CD-ROM containing printable files of worksheets is available. Teachers may print worksheets and distribute them to students for home or school use.

HOW TO USE THIS BOOK

The worksheets in this book facilitate community-based learning for students who have developmental or cognitive disabilities. The purpose of these materials and other materials in the G.A.I.N. (Group Activities for Individual Needs) program is to integrate academic learning with real-life experiences in order to prepare these students to live independently and to get and keep employment in the community.

Many people currently consider community-based learning important not just for students with disabilities but for all students, but proponents of community-based learning don't all agree on the kinds of activities and skills that should be included. The G.A.I.N. program stresses the importance of a broad base of skills, not just skills specifically geared to work situations. Functioning effectively and comfortably in the mainstream of the community involves more than academic and vocational skills. Therefore, the community-based worksheets in this book address skills such as reading signs and maps that foster independence; consumer skills to make independent shopping an option; skills to enhance leisure enjoyment; and skills to promote familiarity with and access to community services. All of these worksheet activities also involve "applied academics," the application of academic skills, such as mathematics and science. Ultimately the skills developed increase the likelihood of obtaining and keeping employment and interpersonal relationships.

In order to maximize learning and enhance appropriate generalization and application of learned skills, learning in the

---

Hospital

HOSPITAL VISIT WORKSHEET - A

During your tour of the hospital you will learn many important things that will be helpful to know if you ever need to go to the hospital. Listen carefully and ask questions about things you see or hear. Fill in the worksheet as you tour the hospital. If you have questions, please ask the tour leader to help you.

1. What is the name of the hospital? _____

2. What is the phone number of the hospital? _____

3. What number should you call if you forget the hospital right away? _____

TOURING THE HOSPITAL LAB

1. What does it feel like to have your blood taken? _____

2. What is the name of the place in the hospital where _____

TOURING THE HOSPITAL X-RAY DEPARTMENT

1. What is the name of the picture that looks inside of _____

2. On what floor is the hospital x-ray department? _____

TOURING THE HOSPITAL FAMILY CARE UNIT

1. Name a reason you would go to the family care unit _____

2. On what floor is the hospital family care unit? _____

NAME: _____

Chapter Six

Community Location's

SIGNS IN THE COMMUNITY - B (worksheet #1)

SIGN	WHERE DID YOU FIND IT?	WRITE THE SIGN HERE
1. FIRE ALARM		
2. BANK		
3. STORE HOURS		
4. HOSPITAL		
5. ONE WAY		
6. ORDER HERE		
7. PRIVATE		
8. ELEVATOR		
9. WET FLOOR		
10. CASHIER		
If you have extra time, find four more signs...		
11.		
12.		
13.		
14.		

NAME: _____ DATE: _____

Chapter Two

Worksheets are provided in three levels of difficulty with A being the easiest and C the most difficult.

"natural environment" is recommended. Therefore, most of the worksheets in this book are to be used on experiential learning outings into the local community. However, because preparation for such outings can often increase the likelihood of successful experiences, some of the worksheets are for classroom use to prepare students for the more authentic community experiences. Other activities, such as writing thank-you letters and book reports, complement the out-of-class experiences but are completed in the classroom.

Like other G.A.I.N. materials, the worksheets in this book present curriculum content at three levels of difficulty. In each case level C is the most difficult of the three and level A is the least demanding. Although level A frequently contains fewer questions than B and B contains fewer questions than C, the number of questions is not the only or the most significant distinction. Questions and tasks at the three levels also vary in degree of complexity. They frequently address different information rather than having the less demanding levels call for "watered down" versions of the more difficult level. Leveling materials is a way of adapting curriculum for students with different abilities. Leveled materials permit the teacher to individualize instruction while still having students work as a group on the same activities. All students have an equal opportunity for meaningful and successful participation in the learning process. There is no assumption that three levels of content difficulty will meet the individual needs of all students at all times and in all subjects. The three levels illustrate the concept; levels can be added or eliminated as appropriate for a particular class or individual student. Although the worksheets in this book were developed for students with disabilities, the leveling concept can be used with students with no identified problems. Leveling is effective at all ages and is particularly useful in inclusive environments.

In addition to the sequence of worksheets, the appendix includes "picture pages" to help students who have significant difficulty reading participate in the community experiences. Picture pages provide step-by-step illustrations for outing rehearsal or follow-up activities.

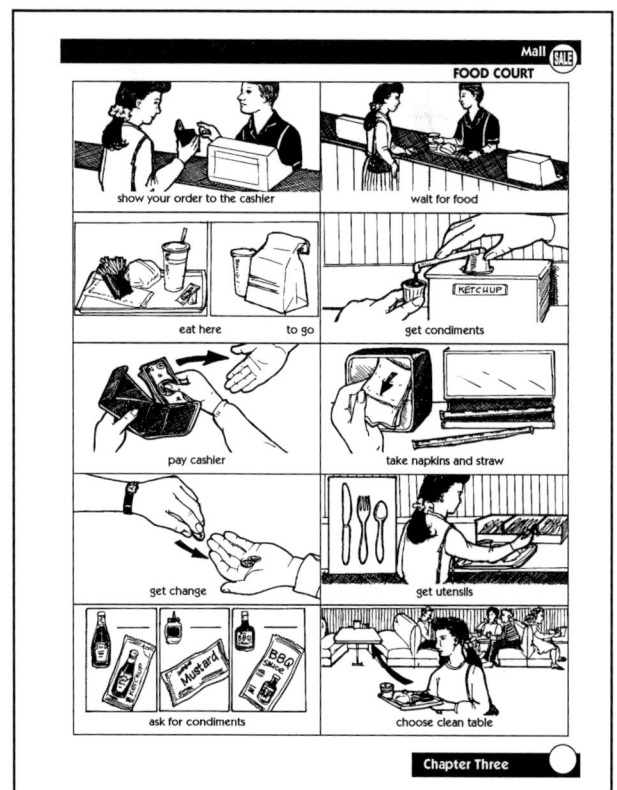

Picture pages illustrate community activities step-by-step.

ORGANIZATION OF THIS BOOK

This book has 26 sets of reproducible worksheets with three levels of difficulty in each set. The worksheets fall generally into the following categories: mobility and self-management (reading signs and maps, cooking); consumer skills (groceries, clothing, and meals); community resources (video store, hospital, library, post office, airport, and zoo visits); and leisure activities (TV, videos, books, and newspapers). There is no attempt to organize the activities by academic subject area since community-based learning is inherently multidisciplinary; various activities require the applied use of mathematics, language arts, social studies, and science. The worksheets also address social skill development and, in some cases, career development.

In addition to the actual worksheets, some supporting materials are included and are found in the appendix of this book. Since the worksheets involve independent living skills in addition to applied academic skills, IEP (Individual Educational Program) objectives and discussion questions related to community-based learning are suggested. (You will also want to develop IEP objectives related to the academic content of the various worksheets, depending upon the individual needs of your particular students.)

The final section also presents an overview of the G.A.I.N. program and a review of recent educational literature related to G.A.I.N. concepts, including the use of community-based learning to maximize preparation for adult life in the community.

THINGS TO CONSIDER IN PLANNING AND CONDUCTING COMMUNITY-BASED LEARNING

Although specific preparation and suggested procedures are discussed in the introduction to each community location, there are some preparations that have to be considered for every outing and will not be repeated in every introduction to the worksheets. In school settings, students cannot be taken off the school grounds without parent permission. Teachers will want to plan well in advance if permission is required for each trip into the community. It is preferable to have a permission form that covers all the outings so that this detail does not have to be a constant concern. Transportation of students to locations beyond walking distance is also a major consideration. Teachers will need to enlist the support of the school administration so that adequate transportation and other support can be provided if needed. In some cases, students may be involved in group projects to raise money for outings.

For many of the community locations included in this book, tours could be arranged for the students. Teachers will want to determine whether or not they would like their students to have tours and to make arrangements well in advance if they do. For locations where tours are not desired, it still might be a good idea to alert the location personnel to the impending visit and perhaps get information about times that would be most convenient for the location and advantageous for the students.

Prior contact with the location personnel could also alert them to any anticipated complicating circumstances, such as the fact that not all students will have money to spend on clothing in the department store. For many of the activities, one teacher may not be sufficient to accompany the group. Depending on the number of students in the group, the ages and individual needs of the students, the type of transportation, and the particular destination, chaperon needs will vary. Teachers will want to make decisions about people needed in time to recruit and, in some cases, brief the volunteers ahead of time. For some of the activities, worksheets require additional information for the particular environment involved; for other activities, teachers may wish to revise and tailor the worksheets to their particular needs.

One of the benefits of community-based learning is exposure to different kinds of environments and to the variations in acceptable behavior in different places. Teachers will want to help students be aware of these expectations and, when important (as in the case of a hospital, for example), the reasons for them. Showing appreciation for these visits to the people involved is an appropriate behavior for students to learn. The worksheets on pages 111–113 can be used for this purpose.

Grocery Shopping

Grocery List Worksheets

Group Grocery List Worksheets

Using the Grocery Advertisements as a Shopping Guide Worksheets

Coupon Savings Worksheets

Locate & Price at the Grocery Worksheets

Amount of Tax You Will Pay at the Store

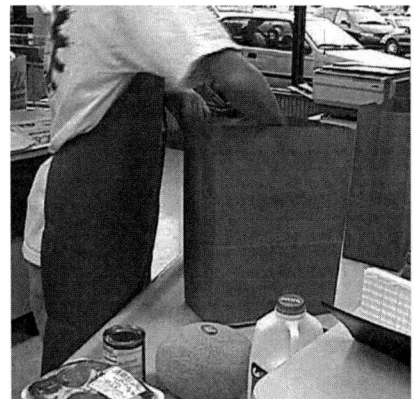

GROCERY SHOPPING INTRODUCTION

People can function independently with greater flexibility and ease if they can manage the grocery store environment. It is anxiety-producing to try to make decisions among large numbers of options in crowded environments where people are frequently in a hurry. Familiarity with the products and the procedures in the store is an intended benefit of the grocery store activities.

Purpose:

To acquaint students with the grocery store and to promote economical and health-conscious food shopping.

Objectives:

Students will begin to understand:

1. How grocery items and foods are categorized.

2. How to plan their purchases before going to the store.

3. How to check item prices.

4. How to use grocery ads to take advantage of specials.

5. How to use grocery coupons.

6. How to estimate total cost of their shopping trip and pay for their purchases.

Academic Curriculum Connections:

Health – Food shopping involves consideration of nutrition and knowledge of food groups.

Language Arts – The worksheets require students to read for specific information. Hopefully, they will also use oral communication skills to obtain information.

Mathematics – The worksheets ask students to estimate their total bill, calculate their bill, compute costs with and without coupons, and practice their money skills.

Preparation and Suggested Procedures:

Before this outing, students will need to learn about food groups. The teacher will want to provide instruction and practice with grocery advertisements and coupons and will need to prepare ad and coupon worksheets ahead of time. Because of the number of tasks, the detail involved, and the pace of the grocery store environment, the student group should be relatively small or several volunteers should be recruited and briefed before the trip.

Students will need to take money, grocery advertisements, and coupons to the store. There are four sets of worksheets for the grocery store outing. The first two sets require students to locate items in the store and record the costs. These will help students become familiar with the store layout before moving on to using grocery ads and, finally, coupons.

GROCERY LIST - A

FOOD TYPE	NAME OF ITEM	NAME OF STORE	COST ($)
MEAT:	1. _____	_____	$.
VEGETABLES:	1. _____	_____	$.
	2. _____		$.
FRUIT:	1. _____	_____	$.
	2. _____		$.
BAKERY:	1. _____	_____	$.
NON-FOOD:	1. _____	_____	$.

NAME: _____ DATE: _____

GROCERY LIST - B

FOOD TYPE	NAME OF ITEM	NAME OF STORE	COST ($)
MEAT:	1. _____	_____	$.
	2. _____	_____	$.
	3. _____	_____	$.
VEGETABLES:	1. _____	_____	$.
	2. _____	_____	$.
	3. _____	_____	$.
FRUIT:	1. _____	_____	$.
	2. _____	_____	$.
	3. _____	_____	$.
DAIRY:	1. _____	_____	$.
	2. _____	_____	$.
BAKERY:	1. _____	_____	$.
	2. _____	_____	$.
NON-FOOD:	1. _____	_____	$.
	2. _____	_____	$.

NAME: _____ DATE:_____

GROCERY LIST - C

FOOD TYPE	NAME OF ITEM	NAME OF STORE	COST ($)
MEAT:	1. _____ 2. _____ 3. _____ 4. _____	_____ _____ _____ _____	$. $. $. $.
VEGETABLES:	1. _____ 2. _____ 3. _____	_____ _____ _____	$. $. $.
FRUIT:	1. _____ 2. _____ 3. _____	_____ _____ _____	$. $. $.
DAIRY:	1. _____ 2. _____	_____ _____	$. $.
BAKERY:	1. _____ 2. _____	_____ _____	$. $.
DELI:	1. _____ 2. _____	_____ _____	$. $.
FROZEN:	1. _____ 2. _____	_____ _____	$. $.
CANNED:	1. _____ 2. _____	_____ _____	$. $.
NON-FOOD:	1. _____ 2. _____	_____ _____	$. $.

NAME: _____ DATE:_____

GROUP GROCERY LIST - A

STUDENT NAME	ITEM	COST
		(#1)
		(#2)
		(#3)

(#1)_____

Copy the cost of each of your items down here and add them together to get a total cost for your group.

(#2)_____

(#3)+_____

Total Number of Items: _____Total Cost of Items: _____

GROUP GROCERY LIST - B

STUDENT NAME	ITEM	COST
	1. _____	_____
	2. _____	_____

subtotal #1 _____

	1. _____	_____
	2. _____	_____

subtotal #2 _____

	1. _____	_____
	2. _____	_____

subtotal #3 _____

Copy the cost of each of your subtotals down here and add them together to get a total cost for your group.

(subtotal #1) _____

(subtotal #2) _____

(subtotal #3)+ _____

Total Number of Items: _____ Total Cost of Items: _____

GROUP GROCERY LIST - C

STUDENT NAME	ITEM	COST
	1. _____ 2. _____ 3. _____ If you have taxable items, put the tax you will owe on this line. ⟶	_____ _____ _____ _____

subtotal #1 _____

	ITEM	COST
	1. _____ 2. _____ 3. _____ If you have taxable items, put the tax you will owe on this line. ⟶	_____ _____ _____ _____

subtotal #2 _____

	ITEM	COST
	1. _____ 2. _____ 3. _____ If you have taxable items, put the tax you will owe on this line. ⟶	_____ _____ _____ _____

subtotal #3 _____

Copy the cost of each of your subtotals down here and add them together to get a total cost for your group.

(subtotal #1) _____

(subtotal #2) _____

(subtotal #3)+ _____

Total Number of Items: _____ Total Cost of Items: _____

USING THE GROCERY ADVERTISEMENTS AS A SHOPPING GUIDE - A

The store advertisement that you will be using today is_____.

PART 1:

How much is… _____? $_____. _____

_____? $_____. _____

_____? $_____. _____

PART 2:

Here is your shopping list…

Buy 1 _____ at $ _____. _____.   This will cost $_____. _____

Buy 1 _____ at $ _____. _____.   This will cost $_____. _____

The cost of these two items will be $_____. _____

Now add the total of the first two items to the cost of the items below

Buy 1 _____ at $ _____. _____.   This will cost $_____. _____

The total cost of your groceries will be $ _____. _____

NAME: _____   DATE:_____

USING THE GROCERY ADVERTISEMENTS AS A SHOPPING GUIDE - B

The store advertisement that you will be using today is_____.

PART 1:

How much is… _____? $_____. _____

_____? $_____. _____

_____? $_____. _____

_____? $_____. _____

_____? $_____. _____

PART 2:

Here is your shopping list…

Buy 1 _____ at $ _____. _____. This will cost $_____. _____

Buy 1 _____ at $ _____. _____. This will cost $_____. _____

Buy 1 _____ at $ _____. _____. This will cost $_____. _____

Buy 2 _____ at $ _____. _____. This will cost $_____. _____

Buy 2 _____ at $_____. _____. This will cost $_____. _____

The total cost of your groceries will be $ _____. _____

NAME:_____ DATE:_____

USING THE GROCERY ADVERTISEMENTS AS A SHOPPING GUIDE - C

The store advertisement that you will be using today is _____.

PART 1:

How much is… _____? $_____ . _____

_____? $_____ . _____

_____? $_____ . _____

_____? $_____ . _____

_____? $_____ . _____

_____? $_____ . _____

_____? $_____ . _____

_____? $_____ . _____

PART 2:

Here is your shopping list…

Buy 1 _____ at $ _____ . _____ . This will cost $_____ . _____

Buy 1 _____ at $ _____ . _____ . This will cost $_____ . _____

Buy 1 _____ at $_____ . _____ . This will cost $_____ . _____

Buy 2 _____ at $ _____ . _____ . This will cost $_____ . _____

Buy 2 _____ at $ _____ . _____ . This will cost $_____ . _____

Buy 2 _____ at $ _____ . _____ . This will cost $_____ . _____

Buy 3 _____ at $ _____ . _____ . This will cost $_____ . _____

Buy 3 _____ at $ _____ . _____ . This will cost $_____ . _____

The total cost of your groceries will be $_____ . _____

NAME: _____ DATE:_____

COUPON SAVINGS - A

Find 4 (four) coupons that you can use for items that are on sale in the grocery store ads in this week's newspaper. Fill in the information below for each coupon that you find.

	The item for which you have a coupon.	The store where the item is on sale.	The cost of the item.	The amount of the coupon.
1.				
2.				
3.				
4.				

NAME: _____ DATE:_____

COUPON SAVINGS - B

Find 8 (eight) coupons that you can use for items that are on sale in the grocery store ads in this week's newspaper. Fill in the information below for each coupon that you find.

	The item for which you have a coupon.	The store where the item is on sale.	The cost of the item.	The amount of the coupon.	The cost using the coupon. (cost-coupon=?)
1.					
2.					
3.					
4.					
5.					
6.					
7.					
8.					

NAME: _____ DATE:_____

COUPON SAVINGS - C

Find 12 (twelve) coupons that you can use for items that are on sale in the grocery store ads in this week's newspaper. Fill in the information below for each coupon that you find.

	The item for which you have a coupon.	The store where the item is on sale.	The cost of the item.	The amount of the coupon.	The cost of using the coupon. (cost-coupon=?)	If the store offers to double the coupon value, what is the cost of the item?
1.						
2.						
3.						
4.						
5.						
6.						
7.						
8.						
9.						
10.						
11.						
12.						

NAME: _____ DATE: _____

LOCATE AND PRICE ITEMS AT THE GROCERY - A

Brand & Size of Item	Location of Item in Store	Item Price	Circle Bill Needed
1.		$.	$ 1.00 $ 5.00 $ 10.00 $ 20.00
2.		$.	$ 1.00 $ 5.00 $ 10.00 $ 20.00
3.		$.	$ 1.00 $ 5.00 $ 10.00 $ 20.00
4.		$.	$ 1.00 $ 5.00 $ 10.00 $ 20.00
5.		$.	$ 1.00 $ 5.00 $ 10.00 $ 20.00

NAME: _____ DATE:_____

LOCATE AND PRICE ITEMS AT THE GROCERY - B

Brand & Size of Item	Location of Item in Store	Item Price	Bill Needed
1.		$.	$.
2.		$.	$.
3.		$.	$.
4.		$.	$.
5.		$.	$.
6.		$.	$.
7.		$.	$.
8.		$.	$.

NAME: _____ DATE:_____

LOCATE AND PRICE ITEMS AT THE GROCERY - C

Brand & Size of Item	Location of Item in Store	Unit Price	Cost of "X" Items	Change from Bill
1.			if "X" = $.	Bill used = $. Change = $.
2.			if "X" = $.	Bill used = $. Change = $.
3.			if "X" = $.	Bill used = $. Change = $.
4.			if "X" = $.	Bill used = $. Change = $.
5.			if "X" = $.	Bill used = $. Change = $.
6.			if "X" = $.	Bill used = $. Change = $.
7.			if "X" = $.	Bill used = $. Change = $.
8.			if "X" = $.	Bill used = $. Change = $.
9.			if "X" = $.	Bill used = $. Change = $.
10.			if "X" = $.	Bill used = $. Change = $.
11.			if "X" = $.	Bill used = $. Change = $.
12.			if "X" = $.	Bill used = $. Change = $.

NAME:_____ DATE:_____

AMOUNT OF TAX YOU WILL PAY AT THE STORE

Use this chart to decide the amount of tax you will have to pay when you buy "taxable" items at the store. Find the amount that is closest to the "price" of the item you want to buy in the left column, and then find the amount of tax you will have to pay listed in the right column. Add the two amounts together to find out the total amount of money you will have to pay the store clerk for the item you want to buy.

FOR STATES THAT HAVE A 5% SALES TAX

AMOUNT OF BILL	AMOUNT OF TAX
$ .50	$ .03
1.00	.05
5.00	.25
7.50	.38
10.00	.50
12.00	.60
15.00	.75
18.00	.90
20.00	1.00
25.00	1.25
30.00	1.50
50.00	2.50

FOR STATES THAT HAVE A 5.5% SALES TAX

AMOUNT OF BILL	AMOUNT OF TAX
$ .50	$ .03
1.00	.06
5.00	.28
7.50	.42
10.00	.55
12.00	.67
15.00	.83
18.00	.99
20.00	1.10
25.00	1.38
30.00	1.65
50.00	2.75

AMOUNT OF TAX YOU WILL PAY AT THE STORE (cont.)

Use this chart to decide the amount of tax you will have to pay when you buy "taxable" items at the store. Find the amount that is closest to the "price" of the item you want to buy in the left column, and then find the amount of tax you will have to pay listed in the right column. Add the two amounts together to find out the total amount of money you will have to pay the store clerk for the item you want to buy.

FOR STATES THAT HAVE A 6% SALES TAX

AMOUNT OF BILL	AMOUNT OF TAX
$ .50	$ .03
1.00	.06
5.00	.30
7.50	.45
10.00	.60
12.00	.72
15.00	.90
18.00	1.08
20.00	1.20
25.00	1.50
30.00	1.80
50.00	3.00

FOR STATES THAT HAVE A 6.5% SALES TAX

AMOUNT OF BILL	AMOUNT OF TAX
$ .50	$ .04
1.00	.07
5.00	.33
7.50	.49
10.00	.65
12.00	.78
15.00	.98
18.00	1.17
20.00	1.30
25.00	1.63
30.00	1.95
50.00	3.25

Local Map Worksheets

Signs in the Community Worksheets

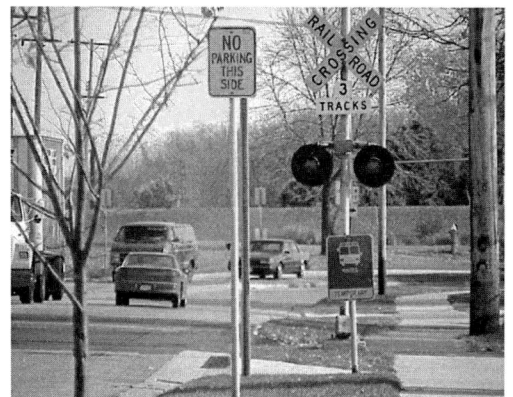

LOCAL COMMUNITY

Students are customarily very well acclimated in their home neighborhoods. Class outings into the community and in-class preparation for these outings are an excellent opportunity to build on this knowledge and broaden skills that can be transferable to other locations. The worksheets for the local community make use of maps of the local area and signs that are commonly encountered.

Purpose:

The purpose of the local community worksheets is to familiarize students with signs commonly encountered in the community and help them learn spatial orientation skills.

Objectives:

Students will:

1. Find specified signs: signs that identify objects and/or services (bank, fire alarm, cashier, police) and signs that convey information and/or directives (store hours, wet floor, no admittance, self-service).

2. Record the locations of the signs found in order to get a sense of the context for the signs.

3. Follow written directions to particular places in the community, identifying landmarks and also following their progress on a map of the area.

Academic Curriculum Connections:

Language Arts – Students will read and write signs and will give verbal directions to each other.

Social Studies – Students will work with maps of the local area.

Social Skills – Students will work together in small groups to complete these tasks.

Preparation and Suggested Procedures:

Teachers will have to create maps of the relevant sections of the local area. Teachers will also need to have knowledge of signs and their locations before tailoring the worksheets to their students. They will need to make decisions about destinations and places along the way in order to complete the worksheet questions. Before going out into the community, the teacher may want to acquaint students with basic maps, perhaps of the school.

Students will want to take maps and instructions on this outing. Teachers and volunteers will need to bring the treats mentioned in the worksheets.

Community Directions

LOCAL MAP - A

Follow the map from school to (the post office). (Insert directions here. For example, ask students to walk "west on Oak Street and turn left onto Maple Street...") As you walk, watch for landmarks along the way.

Fill in this worksheet as you go.

1. What road sign do you see on the corner of (Popular) and (Main) Streets that is NOT a stop sign?

   _____

2. What do you see that is NOT a building on the corner of (College) and (Church) Streets?

   _____

3. What is the name of the school on the corner of (Sycamore) and (Locust) Streets?

   _____

4. What is the name of the restaurant next to the (post office)?

   _____

When you get to the (post office), go inside. You will see (teacher's name) standing by the (postal workers). She/he will have (a treat) for you when you give him/her your completed worksheet.

NAME: _____ DATE:_____

35 **Chapter Two**

LOCAL MAP - B

Follow the map from school to (the post office). (Insert directions here. For example, ask students to walk "west on Oak Street and turn left onto Maple Street...") As you walk, watch for landmarks along the way.

Fill in this worksheet as you go.

1. Is the parking lot on the north side or the south side of (Walnut) Street?

_____

2. (a) Is the local newspaper office on the east side or west side of (Beech) Street?

_____

(b) What is the name of the newspaper office?

_____

3. What is the name of the school on the corner of (Sycamore) and (Locust) Streets?

_____

4. What is the name of the school on the corner of (Smith) Street?

_____

5. What does the sign on the front of the (clothing store) say?

_____

6. What road sign do you see near the corner of (Allen) Road?

_____

When you get to the (post office), go inside. You will see (teacher's name) standing by the (postal workers). She/he will have (a treat) for you when you give him/her your completed worksheet.

NAME: _____ DATE:_____

LOCAL MAP - C

Follow the map from school to (the post office). (Insert directions here. For example, ask students to walk "west on Oak Street and turn left onto Maple Street…") As you walk, watch for landmarks along the way.

Fill in this worksheet as you go.

1. What is the name of the gas station across the road from (Ardmore) Street?

   _____

2. (a) As you walk south on (Harrison) Road, does (Barrel) Street go off to the right or the left?

   _____

   (b) What big building do you see when you look down (Barrel) Street?

   _____

3. What is the name of the school on the corner of (Sycamore) and (Locust) Streets?

   _____

4. What is the name of the movie playing at the (Princess) Theater on (Second) Street?

   _____

5. What road sign other than the stop sign do you see near the intersection of (Green) and (Charles) Streets?

   _____

6. (a) The (GTE) Phone Company Building is on (Church) Street between what two streets?

   _____

   (b) Is the phone company building on the north or south side of (Church) Street?

   _____

7. What two streets do you have to cross if you walk north on (High) Street from (Main) Street to get to the (Star Bank)?

   _____

When you get to the (post office), go inside. You will see (teacher's name) standing by the (postal workers). She/he will have (a treat) for you when you give him/her your completed worksheet.

NAME: _____ DATE: _____

SIGNS IN THE COMMUNITY - A (worksheet #1)

SIGN	WHERE DID YOU FIND IT?	WRITE THE SIGN HERE
1. PUSH		
2. PULL		
3. UP		
4. DOWN		
5. ENTER		
6. EXIT		
7. FIRE		
8. OFFICE		
If you have extra time, find two more signs…		
9.		
10.		

NAME: _____ DATE:_____

SIGNS IN THE COMMUNITY - B (worksheet #1)

SIGN	WHERE DID YOU FIND IT?	WRITE THE SIGN HERE
1. FIRE ALARM		
2. BANK		
3. STORE HOURS		
4. HOSPITAL		
5. ONE WAY		
6. ORDER HERE		
7. PRIVATE		
8. ELEVATOR		
9. WET FLOOR		
10. CASHIER		
If you have extra time, find four more signs…		
11.		
12.		
13.		
14.		

NAME: _____ DATE:_____

SIGNS IN THE COMMUNITY - C (worksheet #1)

SIGN	WHERE DID YOU FIND IT?	WRITE THE SIGN HERE
1. MUNICIPAL BUILDING		
2. THEATER		
3. CONSTRUCTION		
4. RECEPTIONIST		
5. EMERGENCY FIRE ESCAPE		
6. ESCALATOR		
7. PHYSICIAN		
8. RESTAURANT		
9. DRIVE THRU		
10. NO ADMITTANCE		
11. SELF-SERVICE		
12. NO SOLICITING		
If you have extra time, find six more signs…		
13.		
14.		
15.		
16.		
17.		
18.		

NAME: _____ DATE: _____

SIGNS IN THE COMMUNITY - A (worksheet #2)

SIGN	WHERE DID YOU FIND IT?	WRITE THE SIGN HERE
1. IN		
2. OUT		
3. MEN		
4. WOMEN		
5. OPEN		
6. CLOSED		
7. POLICE		
8. NO SMOKING		
If you have extra time, find two more signs…		
9.		
10.		

NAME: _____ DATE: _____

SIGNS IN THE COMMUNITY - B (worksheet #2)

SIGN	WHERE DID YOU FIND IT?	WRITE THE SIGN HERE
1. EMPLOYEES ONLY		
2. DRUGS		
3. EMERGENCY EXIT		
4. DENTIST		
5. DO NOT ENTER		
6. GROCERY		
7. DEAD END		
8. NO PARKING		
9. GENTLEMEN		
10. LADIES		

If you have extra time, find four more signs…

11.		
12.		
13.		
14.		

NAME: _____ DATE:_____

SIGNS IN THE COMMUNITY - C (worksheet #2)

SIGN	WHERE DID YOU FIND IT?	WRITE THE SIGN HERE
1. FIRE EXTINGUISHER		
2. CROSSWALK		
3. EXPRESS CHECKOUT		
4. HARDWARE		
5. RESTRICTED AREA		
6. PROHIBITED		
7. RECEIVING		
8. PHARMACY		
9. AMBULANCE		
10. CORPORATE PARK		
11. COMMUNITY CENTER		
12. DIRECTORY		
If you have extra time, find six more signs…		
13.		
14.		
15.		
16.		
17.		
18.		

NAME: _____ DATE:_____

Locate and Price Clothing Items at the Store Worksheets

Mall Signs Worksheets

Mall Map Worksheets

Mall Meal Purchase Worksheets

SHOPPING MALL

Four sets of worksheets for a mall trip are included, and, of course, many other activities would be possible. Because of its size and complexity, the shopping mall is a good destination to reserve until some less complicated locations have been experienced.

Purpose:

Students will become familiar with a shopping mall, will improve their consumer skills, and will purchase their lunches in the food court.

Objectives:

Students will learn to:

1. Recognize and copy signs commonly found in shopping malls.

2. Identify different kinds of stores and services included in the mall and symbols that represent them.

3. Learn about the kinds of items available in various departments of a store.

4. Read the mall map and use the map to find particular locations.

5. Plan, order, and pay for lunch in the food court, taking cost and nutrition into consideration.

Academic Curriculum Connections:

Mathematics – Students will practice money skills as they pay for their lunches and record the costs.

Language Arts – Students will locate signs and read for information. They will also focus on spelling in order to copy the signs. Students will be encouraged to use oral communication skills by asking mall employees for assistance, as needed.

Social Skills – Students may do some of the activities in groups and will be encouraged to ask for information from mall employees when they need it. They will be encouraged to use appropriate behavior in the Mall.

Health – Students will consider the nutritional value when they are planning their lunch purchases.

Preparation and Suggested Procedures:

Assuming that many of the other outings have been completed before this one, students will have had considerable experience with various kinds of signs and maps before this trip. The teacher may want to plan some lessons related to nutrition of fast foods. Students will need to know about the trip with sufficient time to save or earn lunch money. Rules for the trip will need to be established ahead of time, addressing such things as staying inside the mall and meeting at a particular place and time (perhaps in the food court at lunch time) if students get separated from the whole group.

DEPARTMENT STORE (OR CLOTHING STORE)

Many students will have had experience with clothes shopping, perhaps accompanied by family members.

Department store worksheets concentrate on factors that need to be considered when students shop for clothing for themselves.

Purpose:

Students will learn to shop for clothing appropriate to their needs, taking into consideration size and cost.

Objectives:

Students will:

1. Gain familiarity with departments and locate departments with clothes appropriate to their ages and sizes.

2. Check prices of items of interest.

3. Check sizes and identify their own size.

4. Consider weight and style of clothing and appropriateness for various types of occasions/seasons.

5. Level C students will also look at variations in size from one brand to another.

Academic Curriculum Connections:

Language Arts – Students will have to read for information and may communicate verbally to obtain information.

Social Skills – Students will interact with store employees. They will clarify their personal likes and dislikes.

Mathematics – Students will consider costs of items and total purchases. They will also work within a predetermined budget to gain experience with budgeting.

Social Studies – Students will compare prices and quality, engaging in consumer economics.

Preparation and Suggested Procedures:

If students actually plan to purchase clothing items, they will want to talk with their families ahead of time about particular clothing needs, probable sizes, and cost guidelines. The class will want to talk about store departments that may be of interest and about procedures for locating sizes and using fitting rooms. The teacher may want to contact the store to alert employees to the class visit and the probability that students will want to try on clothes but that some may not be able to make purchases.

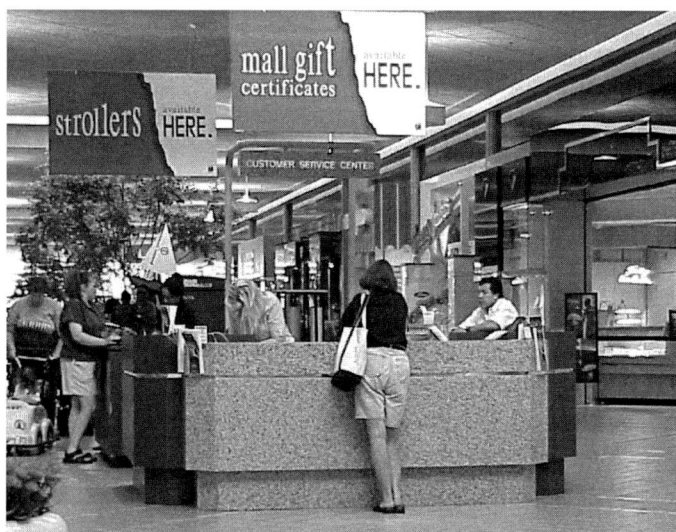

Students considering purchases will need to bring money. They may also want to bring written information about their sizes and clothing needs. The teacher and volunteers will need to be observant and available to be sure that students remember the guidelines for appropriate behavior in the store, especially given that they may be trying on clothing.

If the visit is to a department store, other activities such as shopping for gifts for family members may be added.

LOCATE AND PRICE CLOTHING ITEMS AT THE STORE - A

Name the item.	What size is the item?	Would you wear this when the weather is hot or cold?	How much does the item cost?
			$.
			$.
			$.
			$.
			$.

NAME: _____ DATE:_____

LOCATE AND PRICE CLOTHING ITEMS AT THE STORE - B

Name the item.	What size is the item?	Does the item fit you?	Would you wear the item for work or play?	List the price of the item.
				$.
				$.
				$.
				$.
				$.
				$.
				$.
				$.

NAME: _____ DATE:_____

LOCATE AND PRICE CLOTHING ITEMS AT THE STORE - C

Name the item.	Name the department where this item was found.	What brand and size was the item?	During what time of year would you wear the item?	You might wear this item to go…	What will you pay for the item?
					price $. tax . total $.
					price $. tax . total $.
					price $. tax . total $.
					price $. tax . total $.
					price $. tax . total $.
					price $. tax . total $.
					price $. tax . total $.
					price $. tax . total $.
					price $. tax . total $.
					price $. tax . total $.

NAME: _____ DATE: _____

MALL SIGNS - A

SIGN	LOCATION OF SIGN IN MALL	WRITE THE SIGN HERE
1. EXIT		
2. SALE		
3. MEN		
4. WOMEN		
5. SHOES		
6. RESTROOMS		
7. PHONE		
8. FOOD		
If you have extra time, find three more signs…		
9.		
10.		
11.		

NAME: _____ DATE:_____

MALL SIGNS - B

SIGN	LOCATION OF SIGN IN MALL	WRITE THE SIGN HERE
1. BOYS		
2. GIRLS		
3. NO SMOKING		
4. JEWELRY		
5. NO FOOD OR DRINK		
6. ENTRANCE		
7. ORDER		
8. TOYS		
9. DRUGS		
10. PAY		
11. BOOKS		
12. OFFICE		
13. INFORMATION		
If you have extra time, find three more signs…		
14.		
15.		
16.		

NAME: _____ DATE: _____

MALL SIGNS - C

SIGN	LOCATION OF SIGN IN MALL	WRITE THE SIGN HERE
1. CLEARANCE		
2. SPORTSWEAR		
3. DIRECTORY		
4. JUNIORS		
5. CREDIT OFFICE		
6. TODDLERS		
7. GIFT WRAP		
8. HOUSEWARES		
9. TUXEDOS		
10. COSMETICS		
11. DOMESTICS		
12. CINEMA		
13. CHILDREN		
14. PARKING GARAGE		
15. ACCESSORIES		
If you have extra time, find three more signs…		
16.		
17.		
18.		

NAME: _____ DATE:_____

MALL MAP - A

Use the map to locate stores and find information that will help you in the mall. (Insert the names or numbers that correspond to your local mall map here.) As you fill in each space on this worksheet go to that place in the mall and check to see if your answer is correct.

1. Draw the symbol for the information booth. Go to the information booth and ask what time the mall closes. Write the time here.

   _____

2. How many (shoe) stores are there in the mall?

   _____

3. Draw the symbol for the drinking fountain. Go to the drinking fountain and have a drink of water.

   _____

4. How many public phones are there in the mall? Go to one of the phones. Is there a phone book next to it?

   _____

   Draw the symbol for public phones.

   _____

5. Is there more than one entrance into the mall? Go to one of the entrances and see how many doors are at that entrance. Write the number of doors here.

   _____

   Draw the symbol for mall entrances.

   _____

NAME: _____ DATE:_____

MALL MAP - B

Use the map to locate stores and find information that will help you in the mall. (Insert the names or numbers that correspond to your local mall map here.) As you fill in each space on this worksheet go to that place in the mall and check to see if your answer is correct.

1. Name the largest store in the mall. _____

2. Draw the symbol for money machines that are located in the mall. Go to one of the machines and see what it is called. Write the name here. _____

3. How many (furniture) stores are there in the mall? _____

4. What is the name of store #(26) on the mall map? _____

   What can you buy in this store? _____

5. Draw the symbol for the public restrooms. Is the men's restroom on the left or the right of the women's restroom as you face the doors outside? _____

6. What is the name of store #(45) on the mall map? _____

   What can you buy in this store? _____

7. How many (department) stores are there in the mall? _____

8. Name a street that goes past the mall. _____

NAME: _____ DATE: _____

MALL MAP - C

Use the map to locate stores and find information that will help you in the mall. (Insert the names or numbers that correspond to your local mall map here.) As you fill in each space on this worksheet go to that place in the mall and check to see if your answer is correct.

1. Is the mall located north, south, east, or west of the street that goes past the main entrance? _____

2. How many (drug) stores are there in the mall? _____

3. Draw the symbol for the mall management office. Go to the management office and find out the name of the mall manager. Write the name here. _____

4. What is the name of store #(38) on the mall map? _____
   Would you go to this store? Why? _____

5. How many (clothing) stores are there in the mall? _____

6. What is the name of store #(51) on the mall map? _____
   Would you go to this store? Why? _____

7. Name the smallest store in the mall. _____

8. How many (jewelry) stores are there in the mall? _____

9. Draw the symbol for the mall directory. Go to the directory and find the store that is closest to it. What is the name of the store? _____

10. How many (stationery) stores are there in the mall? _____

11. What is the name of store #(19) on the mall map? _____
    Would you go to this store? Why? _____

12. How many places to eat are there in the mall? _____

NAME: _____   DATE:_____

MALL MEAL PURCHASE WORKSHEET - A

Today, I have $ _____. ___ with me to buy my lunch.

I plan to eat a well-balanced and economical meal at _____.

I will buy: _____, which will cost: $_____. ___

_____, $_____. ___

_____, $_____. ___

I will need _____ one dollar bills to pay for my lunch.

This lunch plan has been approved by _____.

I ate a well balanced and economical lunch today at _____.

I bought: _____, which cost: $_____. ___

_____, $_____. ___

_____, $_____. ___

All together my lunch cost: $_____. ___

Today, I needed to use _____ one dollar bills when I paid for my lunch.

NAME: _____ DATE: _____

MALL MEAL PURCHASE WORKSHEET - B

Today, I have $ _____. ___ with me to buy my lunch.

I plan to eat a well-balanced and economical meal at _____.

I will buy: _____, which will cost: $_____. ___

_____, $_____. ___

_____, $_____. ___

All together my lunch should cost: $_____. ___

This lunch plan has been approved by _____.

I ate a well balanced and economical lunch today at _____.

I bought: _____, which cost: $_____. ___

_____, $_____. ___

_____, $_____. ___

All together my lunch cost: $_____. ___

Today, I got $_____. ___ change back when I paid for my lunch.

NAME: _____ DATE: _____

MALL MEAL PURCHASE WORKSHEET - C

Today, I have $ _____. ___ with me to buy my lunch.

I plan to eat a well-balanced and economical meal at _____.

I will buy: _____, which will cost: $_____. ___

_____, $_____. ___

_____, $_____. ___

_____, $_____. ___

All together my lunch should cost: $_____. ___

Today, I do _____/ do not _____ have enough money with me to pay for my lunch.

This lunch plan has been approved by _____.

I ate a well balanced and economical lunch today at _____.

I bought: _____, which cost: $_____. ___

_____, $_____. ___

_____, $_____. ___

All together my lunch cost: $_____. ___
••••••••••••••

Today, I have $_____. ___ with me to buy my lunch.

I got $_____. ___ change back when I paid for my lunch. (now subtract)

My lunch actually cost $_____. ___. (This should equal the amount you put on the line above the dotted line.)

NAME: _____ DATE:_____

Media

TV Program Guide Worksheets

Video Store Worksheets

*Reading the Newspaper
for Information Worksheets*

Library Worksheets

Library Book Report Worksheets

TV PROGRAM GUIDE

TV program guide worksheets encourage use of a guide primarily for enhancing personal leisure time enjoyment.

Purpose:

Students will learn to read the program schedule and will become familiar with the movie section of the guide.

Objectives:

Students will get exposure to:

1. The kinds of information contained in the program guide.

2. Program schedules and how to read them.

3. And, in the case of level B and level C students, a feature story.

Academic Curriculum Connections:

Language Arts – Students will read the program schedule, movie descriptions, and, in some cases, feature stories.

Social Skills – Students may work in small group on these activities. They will develop their self-assessment skills in the process of considering their preferences.

Preparation and Suggested Procedures:

Teachers will obtain program guides to use in the classroom. Small group work on the activities may enhance motivation and provide good opportunities for socialization and self-awareness skill development.

VIDEO STORE

Watching videotapes is a popular social activity and one that can easily include students at all levels of ability. Helping students gain comfort in negotiating the video rental process will increase their potential for active participation in enjoyable leisure activities.

Purpose:

To acquaint students with video store procedures for renting videos.

Objectives:

Students will learn about:

1. Common categories of videotapes and their interest in the various categories.

2. Video rental costs and late fees.

3. Time limits for video rentals.

4. Appropriate interaction with store employees.

Academic Curriculum Connections:

Language Arts – Worksheet activities require students to read for information and to communicate verbally with store employees. They may also be filling out application forms for video store membership cards.

Mathematics – Students will need to pay for their video rentals, which may include estimating the total amount due in order to have appropriate money ready and counting the change returned.

Social Skills – The video store outing is a good opportunity for students to interact with each other, helping each other locate videos of interest, expressing opinions, and sharing information.

Preparation and Suggested Procedures:

If the video store requires a membership card, students will need to know that in advance and learn how to complete an application for membership. They may also benefit from some assessment of their interests so that they will have ideas about categories of videos they would like to explore and not be overwhelmed by the number of choices.

Students will want to take money for video rentals, and membership cards if they are required. If students will be applying for membership

cards during the visit, they might be advised to bring personal identification and information that is commonly requested on applications for memberships.

A video store is a contained, manageable environment. Students will benefit from sufficient time to browse and socialize in addition to locating videos to rent and completing the worksheet activities.

NEWSPAPER

Students may choose to read newspapers for enjoyment. They also can use newspapers for obtaining information.

Purpose:

Students will learn what is commonly included in newspapers and how to locate sections of interest.

Objectives:

Students will gain skills in:

1. Identifying different sections of the newspaper.

2. Using content guides to locate sections of interest.

3. Reading articles to identify the main ideas and look for specific information.

Academic Curriculum Connections:

Language Arts – Students will read for main ideas and for information and will learn to use content guides.

Social Studies and/or Fine Arts – Depending on the articles that students read, they may also learn content related to social studies (government, economics, history, geography, psychology) or to fine arts (music, theater, art).

Preparation and Suggested Procedures:

At least initially teachers may want to choose the newspapers and bring them to class to be sure that sections are similar and to avoid inappropriate materials for students.

LIBRARY

The library worksheets concentrate on student use of the library for leisure time enjoyment. In addition to becoming familiar with the library and its services, students will choose a fiction book of interest to check out and will follow up the library visit with an in-class book report.

Purpose:

Students will gain practical knowledge for using a public library and will choose a book to read at home or at school and then report on, using the book report worksheets.

Objectives:

Students will become acquainted with:

1. Library location and hours of operation.

2. Procedures for checking out and returning library materials.

3. Penalties for not following library rules.

4. Use of the card catalogue on the computer.

5. Assistance available in the library.

6. Additional services and events at the library.

Students will be able to:

1. Give the title, author, and other objective information about the book they choose.

2. Identify main characters.

3. Form and express opinions about the book.

4. Level B and C students will be expected to provide information about the main characters, and level C students will also be expected to identify the main events in the book.

Academic Curriculum Connections:

Language Arts – Students will read for information, follow directions, learn about the catalog system and organization of books in the library. They will also listen to take in information and will use oral communication skills to ask questions for information. The book report requires identifying main ideas, reading for specific information, and writing several-sentence responses to questions.

Mathematics – Students will consider time periods and money fines.

Computer Skills – Students will use the computerized card catalogue.

Socialization – Students will become aware of activities that take place at the library and that they may want to participate in. They will also interact appropriately with library staff. Making choices about books will enhance their self-awareness and expand options for discussion with peers.

Preparation and Suggested Procedures:

In order to check out library books, students will most likely need library cards. The teacher may want to obtain applications for library cards, help students complete them in class, and be sure that parents have signed them before this outing. In some libraries, it is possible for the teacher to have a special card that can be used for student book check-out, but it is preferable for students to have their own cards and take the responsibility for their books.

Many libraries have their card catalogs available on the internet. If the classroom has computers, the teacher may want to access the card catalog before actually going to the library so that students can become familiar with its use. Some discussion of categories of books would also be helpful. Nonfiction books of interest to students (biographies of sports and rock stars, books about pet care) might be specifically talked about. Since many public libraries have lending items other than books (books on tape, video and audio tapes, games, puppets, magazines), students might be introduced to those options before the library visit.

TV PROGRAM GUIDE WORKSHEET - A

Use the TV program guide to answer the following questions:

1. On what day of the week does the TV program guide begin? _____

2. What is the name of the first TV show listed on Monday evening at "6PM"? _____

   What channel is it on? _____

3. Pick a movie whose name begins with the letter _____ in the movie guide section of the
   TV program guide.

   What is the name of the movie you chose?_____

4. What picture is on the cover of the TV program guide?_____

5. Name one of the channels listed in the TV program guide. _____

NAME: _____ DATE:_____

TV PROGRAM GUIDE WORKSHEET - B

Use the TV program guide to find the following information:

1. What dates does the TV program guide cover? _____

2. What is the name of the TV show that is on channel _____ at 11:30 on Saturday morning?

   _____

3. Pick a movie whose title begins with the letter _____ in the movie guide section of the

   TV program guide.

   Answer the following questions about the movie you chose.

   What day of the week will it be on TV?_____

   What time of day will it be on TV? _____

   What channel will it be on? _____

4. What is the title of the "cover story" which is shown on the front of the TV program guide?

   _____

   What page does the "cover story" begin on? _____

5. Name one of the cable channels listed in the TV program guide. _____

6. What is the name of the TV show that is on channel _____ at 6:00 on Tuesday evening?

   _____

NAME: _____ DATE:_____

TV PROGRAM GUIDE WORKSHEET - C

Use the TV program guide to find the following information:

1. What date is it on the Wednesday that is covered in the TV program guide? _____

2. Find a TV show on Thursday afternoon that you would be interested in watching.

   Answer the following questions about the show you chose:

   What is the name of the show? _____

   What time is it shown? _____ What channel(s) is it on? _____

   What does the TV program guide say about this week's episode of the show? _____

   _____

   _____

   _____

3. Pick a movie whose title begins with the letter _____ in the movie guide section of the

   TV program guide.

   Answer the following questions about the movie you chose:

   What day of the week will it be on TV?_____

   What time of day will it be on TV? _____

   On what channel will it be shown? _____ What TV rating is it given? _____

   What is the movie going to be about? _____

   _____

   _____

   _____

4. Name one of the "premium" channels listed in the TV program guide. _____

   What abbreviation is used to indicate the channel you named? _____

TV PROGRAM GUIDE WORKSHEET - C (cont.)

5. Find a TV show on Monday evening that you would be interested in watching.

    Answer the following questions about the show you chose:

    What is the name of the show? _____

    What time is it shown? _____ What channel(s) is it on? _____

    What does the TV program guide say about this week's episode of the show? _____

    _____

    _____

    _____

6. What is the title of the "cover story" which is shown on the front of the TV program guide?

    _____

    Read the "cover story" in the TV program guide and describe what or who it is about. _____

    _____

    _____

    _____

7. Pick a movie whose title begins with the letter _____ in the movie guide section of the

    TV program guide.

    Answer the following questions about the movie you chose:

    What day of the week will it be on TV?_____

    What time of day will it be on TV? _____

    On what channel will it be shown? _____ What TV rating is it given? _____

    What is the movie going to be about? _____

    _____

    _____

    _____

    _____

NAME: _____ DATE:_____

VIDEO STORE WORKSHEET - A

Pick out three videos that you would like to rent.

Name of the video	What kind of video is it? Circle the correct answer.
1. _____ _____ _____	New releases Comedy Action adventure Drama Science fiction/Horror
2. _____ _____ _____	New releases Comedy Action adventure Drama Science fiction/Horror
3. _____ _____ _____	New releases Comedy Action adventure Drama Science fiction/Horror

NAME: _____ DATE:_____

VIDEO STORE WORKSHEET - B

Pick out four videos that you would like to rent.

Name of the video	What kind of video is it?	When does it have to be returned?	How much will it cost to rent?
1. _____ _____ _____			$.
2. _____ _____ _____			$.
3. _____ _____ _____			$.
4. _____ _____ _____			$.

NAME: _____ DATE: _____

VIDEO STORE WORKSHEET - C

Pick out five videos that you would like to rent.

Name of the video	(a) What kind of video is it? (b) Name one of the actors	What date and time is it due back at the video store?	How much will it cost to rent?	What will it cost to return it late?
1. _____ _____ _____	(a) (b)	date: time:	$.	$.
2. _____ _____ _____	(a) (b)	date: time:	$.	$.
3. _____ _____ _____	(a) (b)	date: time:	$.	$.
4. _____ _____ _____	(a) (b)	date: time:	$.	$.
5. _____ _____ _____	(a) (b)	date: time:	$.	$.

NAME: _____ DATE: _____

READING THE NEWSPAPER FOR INFORMATION - A

Use the newspaper to answer the following questions. (Give each student or small group of students a copy of the local newspaper with this worksheet.)

1. What is the name of the newspaper? _____

2. What does a picture on the front page show? _____

_____

_____

_____

_____

_____

3. Which page has a list of movies being shown near where you live? _____

Write the name of a movie that you would like to see._____

4. Circle the things you can find in this newspaper.

      job ads   comics   weather report   grocery ads   TV program guide

NAME: _____ DATE:_____

READING THE NEWSPAPER FOR INFORMATION - B

Use the newspaper to answer the following questions. (Give each student or small group of students a copy of the local newspaper with this worksheet.)

1. On what date was this newspaper published? _____

2. Read the biggest headline on the front page. What is the story going to be about?

   _____

   _____

   _____

3. What is the title of the first story on page 2? _____

   Who or what is the story about? _____

4. Find another story in the newspaper that interests you and read the first paragraph. What did you learn?

   _____

   _____

   _____

5. Name three kinds of information other than news stories you can find in this newspaper.

   _____

   _____

   _____

NAME: _____ DATE:_____

READING THE NEWSPAPER FOR INFORMATION - C

Use the newspaper to answer the following questions. (Give each student or small group of students a copy of the local newspaper with this worksheet.)

1. Who is the publisher of the newspaper? _____

2. How long has this newspaper been published? _____

3. Read the first paragraph on page one of the newspaper and answer the following questions.
   What is the event that took place?_____
   When did it happen? _____
   Who wrote the article?_____

4. Find an article inside the newspaper that interests you and read it.
   Title _____Author _____
   What is the most important thing you learned from reading this story?
   _____
   _____

5. Find another article inside the newspaper that interests you and read it.
   Title _____Author _____
   List the major events that took place in the story in the order in which they occurred.
   _____
   _____
   _____
   _____

6. List the names of different sections in this newspaper and describe the kinds of information that is found in each section.

Section Name	Kinds of Information
_____	_____
_____	_____
_____	_____

NAME: _____ DATE:_____

LIBRARY WORKSHEET - A

USING THE LIBRARY:

1. What is the name of the library?_____

2. What day(s) of the week is the library closed? _____

3. Who can you ask to help you find a book?_____

4. Where do you return the books you borrow from the library?_____

_____

5. What do you have to have before you can check out a library book? Circle the answer.

          a. money   b. library card

GETTING HELP:

1. Ask for help to find a book about (topic of interest to the student). Write the name of the book you

   find here._____

NAME: _____ DATE:_____

LIBRARY WORKSHEET - B

USING THE LIBRARY:

1. Where is the library located? _____

2. What days of the week is the library open? _____
   _____

3. Answer the following questions about borrowing library books:

   a. How many days can you keep a library book? _____

   b. What happens if you keep the book longer? _____

   c. What happens if you lose the book you've borrowed? _____

4. Use the computer terminal to find (title of a book the student will enoy reading).

   a. What is the name of the book's author(s)? _____

   b. Where is it in the library? _____

GETTING HELP:

1. Are there any special events that sometimes take place at the library? _____

   If so, what are they? _____
   _____

2. Where can I return books when the library is closed? _____

NAME: _____   DATE: _____

LIBRARY WORKSHEET - C

USING THE LIBRARY:

1. What is the library call number on the book? _____

2. In what section of the library did you find the book? _____

3. What can you borrow from the library in addition to books? _____
   _____

4. a. What are the library's usual hour of operation? _____
   b. Are there any days of the week when the library is open during different hours? _____
   c. If so, what day(s) and what are those hours of operation? _____

5. How much is the daily fee for each book that is overdue? _____

6. Pick a subject that interests you. _____
   Use the computer terminal to find a book on that subject.
   a. What is the title of the book? _____
   b. What is the author's name? _____
   c. Now find another title by the same author. _____

GETTING HELP:

1. Ask the librarian about story times/lectures you can attend. With the information you learn from the librarian, answer the following questions:
   a. Do they happen on a regular basis? _____
   b. If so, what are they and when are they offered? _____
   _____
   c. What is the next event that is offered? _____
   d. What date and time is the next scheduled event? _____

2. Can I renew a library book without going to the library? _____
   If so, how can I do it? _____

NAME: _____ DATE: _____

LIBRARY BOOK REPORT WORKSHEET - A

Choose a book from the library that you would like to read.

Carefully read the book you have chosen and ask questions when you have trouble reading a word or do not understand something you read. Fill in this worksheet when you finish reading the book. If you are not sure how to answer any of the worksheet questions, please ask the teacher to help you.

1. What is the name of the book? _____

2. Who wrote the book? _____

3. How many pages are there in the book?_____

4. Who are the main characters in the book? _____

   _____

5. Did you like the book? _____

   If so, why did you like it; or if not, why not?_____

   _____

   _____

NAME: _____ DATE:_____

LIBRARY BOOK REPORT WORKSHEET - B

Choose a book from the library that you would like to read.

Carefully read the book you have chosen and ask questions when you have trouble reading a word or do not understand something you read. Fill in this worksheet when you finish reading the book. If you are not sure how to answer any of the worksheet questions, please ask the teacher to help you.

1. What is the title of the book? _____

2. Who is (are) the author(s) of the book? _____

3. Are there chapters in the book? _____

   If so, how many are there? (Look for the answer in the table of contents.) _____

4. Did the book have a happy or a sad ending? _____

5. List the main characters in the book and write a sentence about each of them. _____

   _____

   _____

   _____

   _____

   _____

LIBRARY BOOK REPORT WORKSHEET - B (cont.)

6. Write a paragraph that tells what happened in the book._____

_____

_____

_____

_____

_____

_____

_____

_____

_____

7. What did you like about the book, and why?_____

_____

_____

_____

_____

_____

_____

_____

_____

_____

_____

NAME: _____ DATE:_____

LIBRARY BOOK REPORT WORKSHEET - C

Choose a book from the library that you would like to read.

Carefully read the book you have chosen and ask questions when you have trouble reading a word or do not understand something you read. Fill in this worksheet when you finish reading the book. If you are not sure how to answer any of the worksheet questions, please ask the teacher to help you.

1. What is the title of the book? _____

2. Who is (are) the author(s) of the book?_____

3. What is the copyright date of the book? _____

4. Who is the publisher of the book? _____

5. Does this book have a table of contents? _____

   If so, where is it located in the book? _____

   What kind of information do you find in the table of contents?_____

   _____

   _____

   _____

   _____

LIBRARY BOOK REPORT WORKSHEET - C (cont.)

6. Who are the main female characters in the book and why are they important to the story?_____

_____

_____

_____

_____

7. Who are the main male characters in the book and why are they important to the story? _____

_____

_____

_____

_____

8. Which character did you like best and why? _____

_____

_____

_____

_____

9. What was the most important thing that happened in the book? _____

_____

_____

Who did it happen to and why was it important? _____

_____

_____

LIBRARY BOOK REPORT WORKSHEET - C (cont.)

10. What did you like best about this book?_____

_____

_____

_____

_____

_____

_____

_____

_____

_____

11. What did you like least about this book?_____

_____

_____

_____

_____

_____

_____

_____

_____

_____

NAME: _____ DATE:_____

Recipe Planning Worksheets

RECIPE PLANNING

Recipe planning is a daily living skill and can also be an enjoyable leisure-time activity.

Purpose:

To help students learn to read recipes with understanding so that they can successfully follow recipes when cooking.

Objectives:

Students will learn about:

1. Different kinds of ingredients and proper handling of them.

2. Cooking temperatures and times.

3. Measurement of ingredients.

4. Following directions in a sequential manner.

5. Recipes in the context of meal planning and healthy eating.

6. Estimating time needed to assemble and prepare various recipes.

Academic Curriculum Connection:

Health – Students will consider nutrition and safe handling and storage of foods.

Mathematics – Students will measure ingredients, and will use multiplication or addition to double or halve recipes. They will also practice time skills and add amounts of time to estimate total time for recipe preparation.

Language Arts – Students will read carefully for step by step instructions.

Preparation and Suggested Procedures:

At least initially, teachers will want to select recipes so that they are appropriate to students' skill and developmental levels. Volunteers may be needed to help groups of students with measuring activities. Measuring implements and ingredients will need to be provided.

RECIPE PLANNING - A

Use the recipe your teacher has given you to answer the following questions. (A separate sheet containing a simple recipe should accompany this worksheet. The recipe page should show a recipe with no more than four ingredients, no more than three steps to prepare the recipe, and a picture of how the prepared recipe will look.)

1. How many people does your recipe serve?_____

2. What is the "main ingredient" in your recipe? _____

3. How many different ingredients are there in your recipe? _____

4. How do you think your recipe will taste? Will it taste sweet (hot, juicy, salty), or will it taste some

   other way? _____

5. Do you think you will want to eat the food your recipe makes? _____

   Why? _____

NAME: _____ DATE:_____

RECIPE PLANNING - B

Use the recipe your teacher has given you to answer the following questions. (A separate sheet containing a simple recipe should accompany this worksheet. The recipe page should show a recipe with no more than seven ingredients, no more than six steps to prepare the recipe, and a picture of how the prepared recipe will look.)

1. For what part of the meal would you serve this recipe?_____

2. In this recipe, how much of the second ingredient do you need? _____

3. Does this recipe require cooking? _____

   If so, at what temperature do you need to set the oven?_____

4. Which ingredients in this recipe are liquids?_____

   _____

5. Which ingredients in this recipe need to be refrigerated? _____

   _____

6. Which step in the recipe do you think will take the most time to do?_____

   Why? _____

7. Give the amounts needed for each ingredient if you double this recipe. _____

   _____

   _____

   _____

NAME: _____ DATE:_____

RECIPE PLANNING - C

Use the recipe your teacher has given you to answer the following questions. (A separate sheet containing a simple recipe should accompany this worksheet. The recipe page should show a recipe with no more than ten ingredients, no more than nine steps to prepare the recipe, and a picture of how the prepared recipe will look.)

1. How much time should you allow to prepare this recipe? _____

2. List the "dry" ingredients in this recipe. _____
_____

3. If there are leftovers, where should you store them? _____

4. What equipment will you need to use when you make this recipe? _____
_____

5. How much of the sixth ingredient is needed if you triple this recipe? _____

6. Which step in this recipe do you think will be the hardest?_____
Why? _____

7. How much of the fourth ingredient is needed if you double this recipe? _____

8. Does this recipe need to be cooked?_____
If so, how much time should you allow for it to cook? _____
Be sure to add 10 minutes to the time you plan for cooking to let the oven "preheat."

9. Give the amounts needed for each ingredient if you make only half of this recipe. _____
_____
_____
_____

NAME: _____ DATE:_____

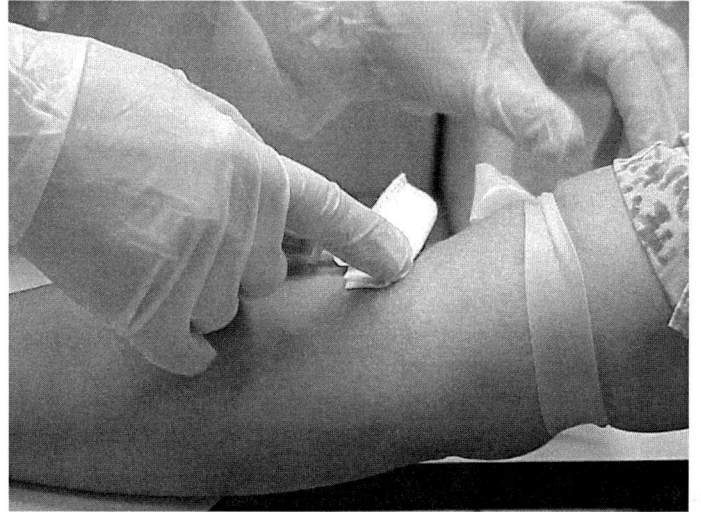

Hospital Visit Worksheets

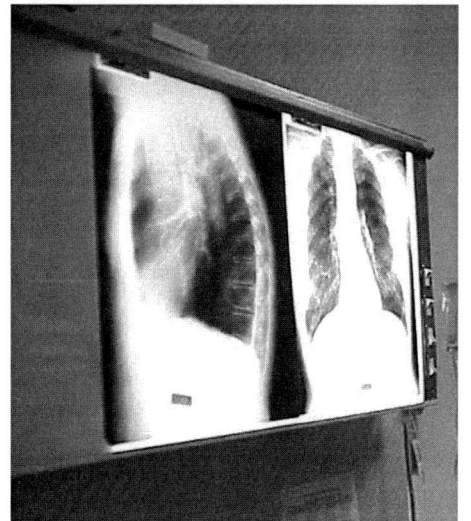

HOSPITAL

The hospital visit is the only one of the community-based learning outings that requires a tour since students cannot have access to most hospital departments without one. The hospital visit will begin to familiarize students with hospital departments and services so that they will be less anxious and more knowledgeable when they themselves or people they know need hospital services.

Purpose:

To acquaint students with outpatient departments and services and increase their comfort level in the hospital environment.

Objectives:

Students will tour some outpatient departments with a hospital employee and will learn:

1. How to access local hospital services.

2. What is done in the laboratory, the x-ray department, and the "convenient care" area ("family care" or other name may be used in different hospitals).

3. How to access medical care in case of an emergency.

4. Appropriate behavior for a non-patient in a hospital.

5. Level C worksheets request additional information about possible needs for various services, about bill-paying, and about hospital jobs.

Academic Curriculum Connections:

Science – The laboratory and x-ray areas are examples of applied sciences, which can be excellent adjuncts to units on the human skeleton or body systems.

Health – Students will gain knowledge of preventive care and treatment of illnesses.

Language Arts – Students will be expected to listen carefully and take in information orally. They will also be encouraged to ask questions.

Social Skills – Students will be learning to interact appropriately with a tour leader and to behave appropriately in a hospital.

Preparation and Suggested Procedures:

Students will benefit more from their hospital visit if they have studied body systems, health care procedures, and various illnesses and diagnostic tests. They will understand the need for quiet and careful behavior if they have discussed it in class before going to the hospital.

The teacher will want to make arrangements with the hospital well in advance so that students can have a tour. Although the worksheets do not include specific questions about these areas, the tour might include an introduction to the admissions area and the information desk.

HOSPITAL VISIT WORKSHEET - A

During your tour of the hospital you will learn many important things that will be helpful to know if you ever need to go to the hospital. Listen carefully and ask questions when you do not understand something you see or hear. Fill in the worksheet as you tour the hospital. If you are not sure how to answer any of the questions, please ask the tour leader to help you.

1. What is the name of the hospital? _____

2. What is the phone number of the hospital? _____

3. What number should you call if you forget the hospital number and you need medical help

   right away? _____

TOURING THE HOSPITAL LAB

1. What does it feel like to have your blood taken? _____

2. What is the name of the place in the hospital where you go to have your blood taken?

   _____

TOURING THE HOSPITAL X-RAY DEPARTMENT

1. What is the name of the picture that looks inside of your body?_____

2. On what floor is the hospital x-ray department?_____

TOURING THE HOSPITAL FAMILY CARE UNIT

1. Name a reason you would go to the family care unit. _____

2. On what floor is the hospital family care unit? _____

NAME: _____ DATE:_____

HOSPITAL VISIT WORKSHEET - B

During your tour of the hospital you will learn many important things that will be helpful to know if you ever need to go to the hospital. Listen carefully and ask questions when you do not understand something you see or hear. Fill in the worksheet as you tour the hospital. If you are not sure how to answer any of the questions, please ask the tour leader to help you.

1. What is the name of the hospital? _____

2. On what street is the hospital? _____

3. What is the phone number of the hospital? _____

4. What is the name of the person who is showing you the hospital?_____

   What is that person's regular job in the hospital? _____

TOURING THE HOSPITAL LAB

1. Why would you go to the hospital lab? _____

2. On what floor is the hospital lab? _____

3. Why might a doctor need to test your blood? _____

TOURING THE HOSPITAL X-RAY DEPARTMENT

1. Name a reason that you might have an x-ray. _____

2. What does an x-ray show the doctor?_____

   _____

HOSPITAL VISIT WORKSHEET - B (cont.)

TOURING THE HOSPITAL FAMILY CARE UNIT

1. What are two reasons that might cause you to go to the family care unit?

   a. _____

   b._____

2. How would you make an appointment at the family care unit?_____

   _____

3. On what floor is the hospital family care unit? _____

NAME: _____ DATE:_____

HOSPITAL VISIT WORKSHEET - C

During your tour of the hospital you will learn many important things that will be helpful to know if you ever need to go to the hospital. Listen carefully and ask questions when you do not understand something you see or hear. Fill in the worksheet as you tour the hospital. If you are not sure how to answer any of the questions, please ask the tour leader to help you.

1. What is the full name and address of the hospital?_____

_____

_____

2. What is the phone number of the hospital pharmacy? _____

3. Name two reasons for which you might need to go to the hospital?

   a. _____

   b. _____

4. How can you find which department you need to go to when you get to the hospital?_____

_____

5. Where do you pay your hospital bill? _____

TOURING THE HOSPITAL LAB

1. Name two things that happen in a hospital lab.

   a. _____

   b. _____

2. What kind of test uses what looks like a long Q-tip that is rubbed on the back of the throat?

_____

3. What kind of instrument does the lab technician look into to make cells appear large enough to see?

_____

HOSPITAL VISIT WORKSHEET - C (cont.)

4. What color is your blood? _____

5. Name a body fluid other than saliva or blood that might need to be looked at in the hospital lab.

   _____

TOURING THE X-RAY DEPARTMENT

1. What kind of doctor looks at x-rays? _____

   a. What do you think doctors did to find out what was wrong inside a person's body before there

      were x-rays? _____

   b. Now that there are x-rays, do they still have to do this sometimes? _____

      Why? _____

TOURING THE FAMILY CARE UNIT

1. Why do you choose to go to the family care unit instead of another department in the hospital?

   _____

2. Who will take care of you at the family care unit?_____

3. What does a visit to the family care unit cost? _____

4. Name a reason that the family care unit would not be the right place to go if you needed medical

   care. _____

NAME: _____ DATE:_____

Zoo

Zoo Worksheets

ZOO

The zoo outing is different from most other outings in the book because knowledge of the zoo is not necessary for living independently and is less crucial to socializing than the mall or the video store. However, in most areas zoos are relatively inexpensive, highly enjoyable leisure-time choices for all ages. They are also an effective science activity and provide another opportunity to practice spatial-orientation skills and observe signs.

Purpose:

The zoo worksheets will acquaint students with a large variety of animals and their habitats and habits in a popular leisure-time environment.

Objectives:

Students will:

1. Identify different kinds of animals.

2. Learn what various animals eat, how they move, and what kinds of homes they have.

3. Use zoo maps to locate various animals.

4. Level B students will also learn about the skin of various animals.

5. Level C students will learn the area of the world and the kind of habitat each animal comes from and about animals' means of protection.

Academic Curriculum Connections:

Science – The identification and observation of the various animals and all of the specific information about their habitats and habits fit into biological science.

Social Studies – Map reading will be part of this outing. Also, students, especially those at the C level, will be exposed to geographical information about the animals.

Language Arts – Students will locate signs and read for information.

Social Skills – At least part of the time, students will be operating in small groups and socializing with each other while they complete the activities.

Preparation and Suggested Procedures:

The trip to the zoo is probably the most expensive community-based learning activity in this book. Arrangements for covering the expense of the trip will need to be made well in advance. Perhaps the students could be involved in a fund-raising activity. Students will benefit from this outing more if they have knowledge about animals before going. The trip might even focus on particular animals that have been studied, especially if students will have more than one opportunity to visit the zoo during their school years. Guidelines for the trip will need to be established with the students ahead of time, dealing with such topics as safety considerations, degree of autonomy allowed, meal plans, and time at the zoo.

If the teacher wants to take advantage of particular events or arrange for any special tours (for example, "behind the scenes" tours of the nursery or hospital) or educational presentations, prior arrangements with zoo personnel will be necessary.

Students will need to bring money and/or food on this trip and may wish to bring cameras.

ZOO VISIT WORKSHEET - A

1. What is the name of the zoo? _____

2. When you see one of the animals listed below, put a check by that animal on the chart.
   Fill in the chart while you watch the animal.

What kind of animal is it?	How does it move?	What does it like to eat?	Where does it sleep?
1. **elephant** check_____			
2. **snake** check_____			
3. **monkey** check_____			
4. **bird** check_____			
5. **fish** check_____			

NAME: _____ DATE:_____

ZOO VISIT WORKSHEET - B

1. What is the phone number at the zoo? _____

2. How much does it cost adults to go to the zoo? _____

3. How much does it cost children to go to the zoo? _____

4. When you see one of the animals listed below, put a check by that animal on the chart.
   Fill in the chart while you watch the animal.

What kind of animal is it?	How does it go from place to place?	What kind of food does it eat?	What kind of skin does it have?	What kind of home does it have?
1. **lion** check_____				
2. **bear** check_____				
3. **ape** check_____				
4. **spider** check_____				

ZOO VISIT WORKSHEET - B (cont.)

What kind of animal is it?	How does it go from place to place?	What kind of food does it eat?	What kind of skin does it have?	What kind of home does it have?
5. **duck** check_____				
6. **bat** check_____				
7. **alligator** check_____				
8. **zebra** check_____				
9. **hippo** check_____				
10. **seal** check_____				

NAME: _____ DATE: _____

ZOO VISIT WORKSHEET - C

1. How much does a season pass cost an individual? $ _____.____

2. How many visits does the individual have to make in a year for the season pass to be less expensive than paying for admission each time the individual visits the zoo?   _____visits

3. How much does a season pass cost a family? $ _____.____

4. How many visits does a family of (# of people) have to make in a year for the season pass to be less expensive than paying for admission each time the family visits the zoo?   _____visits

5. When you see one of the animals listed below, put a check by that animal on the chart. Fill in the chart while you watch the animal.

What kind of animal is it?	What kind of locomotion does it use?	Describe its diet.	How does it protect itself from its enemies?	Describe its habitat.	What part of the world does it come from?
1. **shark** check _____					
2. **beetle** check _____					
3. **rhinoceros** check _____					
4. **zebra** check _____					
5. **penguin** check _____					

ZOO VISIT WORKSHEET - C (cont.)

What kind of animal is it?	What kind of locomotion does it use?	Describe its diet.	How does it protect itself from its enemies?	Describe its habitat.	What part of the world does it come from?
6. **tiger** check _____					
7. **turtle** check _____					
8. **camel** check _____					
9. **chimpanzee** check _____					
10. **ostrich** check _____					
11. **dolphin** check _____					
12. **giraffe** check _____					
13. **goat** check _____					
14. **swan** check _____					
15. **eagle** check _____					

NAME: _____ DATE: _____

Thank You Letter Worksheets

Post Office Visit Worksheets

POST OFFICE

Not everyone writes letters, but almost everyone pays bills, files tax information, moves, receives packages, and receives junk mail. In order to function independently, students need to be familiar with the post office and at least some of its services. Students can also benefit from exposure to the kinds of jobs available in the postal system.

Purpose:

The purpose of the post office worksheets is to make students aware of services and help them become comfortable accessing services.

Objectives:

Students will be able to:

1. Purchase stamps.

2. Ask for information about different kinds of mailing options.

3. Know of other services provided by the post office.

4. Gain knowledge of forms available in the post office and understand what they are for and how to complete them. Level A includes a form for requesting that mail be held, level B includes a registration form for selective service, and level C includes a packet of information for moving, with a change of address form.

Academic Curriculum Connections:

Social Studies – Students will be learning about government services.

Language Arts – Students will use oral communication skills to request information from postal employees. They will read and complete forms.

Mathematics – Students will learn about postal costs and stamp vending machine costs.

Social Skills – Students will learn to interact appropriately with postal employees.

Preparation and Suggested Procedures:

Teachers may want to prepare students for their post office visit by providing information about different stamp values (letters, postcards, etc.) and about different mailing options, such as priority mail. Students should also have some exposure to filling out forms before filling out post office forms.

The post office will provide tours for interested groups. The teacher will want to decide whether or not to include a tour in the post office visit.

THANK YOU LETTER - A

(Date) _____

Dear _____,

Thank you very much for letting me visit_____.

I really enjoyed myself. The thing I liked best was _____

because _____

_____.

Thank you again.

Sincerely,

(Name) _____

NAME: _____ DATE:_____

THANK YOU LETTER - B

(Date) _____

Dear _____,

   Thank you for _____.

I really liked _____.

The most interesting thing I learned during my visit was_____

_____.

It was particularly interesting to me because _____

_____.

   Thank you again for _____.

I wish I could have taken more time to _____

while I was there. I hope I can visit _____ again soon.

Sincerely,

(Name) _____

NAME: _____ DATE:_____

THANK YOU LETTER - C

_____

_____/

_____

_____

_____

_____.

_____

_____

_____

_____.

_____

_____.

_____/

_____

NAME: _____ DATE:_____

POST OFFICE VISIT WORKSHEET - A

1. What street is the post office on? _____

2. What do you buy at the post office to put on a letter? _____

3. Who delivers the mail? _____

4. What time does the post office open? _____

5. Find the mailbox outside of the post office.

   What time is the mail picked up on Monday?_____

6. a) Is there a vending machine in the post office where you can buy stamps after the regular post

   office closes? _____

   b) How much money do you need to buy a stamp from the vending machine?_____

7. Ask the postal worker for an "Authorization to Hold Mail" form.

   Bring it back to the school and fill it out in class.

NAME: _____ DATE:_____

POST OFFICE VISIT WORKSHEET - B

1. What street is the post office on? _____

2. Who works at the post office? _____

3. Name three things you can do at the post office.

   _____

   _____

   _____

4. How much does a postcard stamp cost? _____

5. Find the mailbox outside of the post office.

   What time is the mail picked up on Tuesday? _____

   What time is the mail picked up on Saturday? _____

6. When does the post office open on Wednesday? _____

   When does the post office close on Wednesday? _____

   When does the post office open on Saturday? _____

   When does the post office close on Saturday? _____

7. Is there a vending machine in the post office where you can buy stamps after the regular post office

   closes? _____

   What stamps do you get from the vending machine when you insert ($.35)?_____

   How many letters can you mail with these stamps? _____

8. Find or ask the postal worker for a "Selective Service System Registration" form.

   Bring it with you when you return to the school and fill it out in class.

NAME: _____ DATE:_____

POST OFFICE VISIT WORKSHEET - C

1. Where is the post office located? Give the complete address. _____

   _____

   _____

2. Who owns the post office? _____

3. Name four things other than stamps for letters or postcards that you can buy at the post office and

   list the cost of each item.

   _____cost: _____

   _____cost: _____

   _____cost: _____

   _____cost: _____

4. What is registered mail? _____

5. What is certified mail? _____

6. Find the deposit letter slots inside the post office.

   Do you have a choice of "in town" and "out of town" mail slots? _____

   What zip code(s) indicate(s) "in town" mail? _____

7. When is the post office open?

   Full Days: _____Hours: _____

   Partial Days: _____Hours: _____

POST OFFICE VISIT WORKSHEET - C (cont.)

8. Is there a vending machine in the post office where you can buy stamps after the regular post office

closes? _____

What stamps do you get from the vending machine when you insert ($1.00)?_____

How many letters can you mail with these stamps? _____

What stamps do you get from the vending machine when you insert ($1.65)?_____

How many letters can you mail with these stamps? _____

9. Find or ask the postal worker for a "Mover's Guide" booklet that contains a "Change of Address" card.

Bring it with you when you return to the school and fill it out in class.

NAME: _____ DATE:_____

Transportation

Airport Flight Arrival & Departures Worksheets

Airport Signs Worksheets

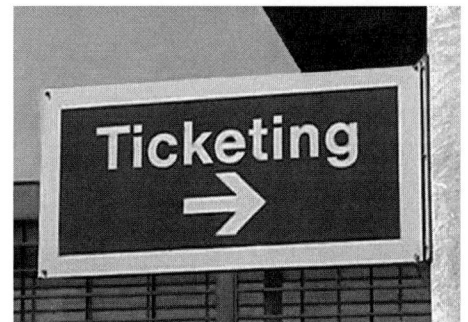

AIRPORT

Students may accompany travelers to or from the airport and will want to feel comfortable and competent in the environment whether or not they actually become air travelers. These worksheets do not focus on preparing students to be air travelers.

Purpose:

The purpose of the airport worksheets is to acquaint the students with vocabulary, places, and procedures that are peculiar to airports.

Objectives:

Students will be exposed to:

1. Signs frequently found in airports.

2. Arrival and departure boards and how to read and understand the information shown on them.

3. Important places, such as the baggage claim area and gates.

4. Security procedures for approaching gate areas.

5. Other services and amenities often available at airports.

Academic Curriculum Connections:

Mathematics – Students will read times and will calculate waiting times before planes are expected to arrive or depart.

Language Arts – The worksheets require students to locate signs in the airport and to read information from flight arrival and departure boards and maps of the airport.

Preparation and Suggested Procedures:

Teachers may want to change some of the time and gate questions on the worksheets after seeing the arrival and departure boards so that students will not have long waits to get information requested about arriving and departing flights. Before taking students to the airport, the teacher may want to teach them to read arrival and departure information. Explanations of security procedures and the reasons for them would also be helpful before students are confronted with security gates at the airport.

Students will want to take picture identification in case it is required to pass through security. If they are planning to eat at the airport, they will need money.

AIRPORT FLIGHT ARRIVAL AND DEPARTURES - A

A. Find the flight **arrival** chart in the airport terminal. Look at the chart and answer the following questions.

    1. What is the number of the 1st flight listed on the chart?   Flight: #_____

       What gate should you go to for this flight?   Gate: #_____

       What time should it arrive?   Time: _____

    2. What is the number of the 2nd flight listed on the chart?   Flight: #_____

       What gate should you go to for this flight?   Gate: #_____

       What time should it arrive?   Time: _____

B. Now, find the flight **departure** chart. Look at the chart and answer the following questions.

    1. What is the number of the 1st flight listed on the chart?   Flight: #_____

       What gate should you go to for this flight?   Gate: #_____

       What time should it leave?   Time: _____

    2. What is the number of the 2nd flight listed on the chart?   Flight: #_____

       What gate should you go to for this flight?   Gate: #_____

       What time should it leave?   Time: _____

C. Now, go to Gate 1 and watch the next plane as it lands. First, you have to go through the security check point. Name one thing you see people put in the small bowl before they walk through the security gate.

_____

AIRPORT FLIGHT ARRIVAL AND DEPARTURES - B

A. Find the flight **arrival** chart in the airport terminal. Look at the chart and answer the following questions.

1. What is the number of the 2nd flight listed on the chart?   Flight: #_____

   What airline is it?   Airlines: _____

   Where is it coming from?   Place: _____

   At which gate will it arrive?   Arrival gate: _____

2. What is the number of the 6th flight listed on the chart?   Flight: #_____

   What airline is it?   Airlines: _____

   Where is it coming from?   Place: _____

   At which gate will it arrive?   Arrival gate: _____

B. Now, find the flight **departure** chart. Look at the chart and answer the following questions.

1. What is the number of the 5th flight listed on the chart?   Flight: #_____

   What airline is it?   Airlines: _____

   Where is it going?   Place: _____

   Which gate will it depart from?   Departure gate: _____

2. What is the number of the 8th flight listed on the chart?   Flight: #_____

   What airline is it?   Airlines: _____

   Where is it going?   Place: _____

   Which gate will it depart from?   Departure gate: _____

C. Now, go to Gate 2 and watch the arrival of the next flight. First, you must pass through the security check point. What happens if a noise sounds when someone walks through the security gate?

_____

NAME: _____ DATE:_____

AIRPORT FLIGHT ARRIVAL AND DEPARTURES - C

A. Find the flight **arrival** chart in the airport terminal. Look at the chart and answer the following questions.

1. What is the number of the 3rd flight listed on the chart?   Flight: # _____

   What time is the flight due to arrive?   Time: _____

   What is the arrival status of the flight?   Status: _____

   How long do you have to wait until the plane arrives?   Arrival time: _____

   Present time: - _____

   Wait time: _____

2. What is the number of the 11th flight listed on the chart?   Flight: # _____

   What time is the flight due to arrive?   Time: _____

   What is the arrival status of the flight?   Status: _____

   How long do you have to wait until the plane arrives?   Arrival time: _____

   Present time: - _____

   Wait time: _____

3. What is the number of the 8th flight listed on the chart?   Flight: # _____

   What time is the flight due to arrive?   Time: _____

   What is the arrival status of the flight?   Status: _____

   How long do you have to wait until the plane arrives?   Arrival time: _____

   Present time: - _____

   Wait time: _____

AIRPORT FLIGHT ARRIVAL AND DEPARTURES - C (cont.)

B. Now, find the flight **departure** chart. Look at the chart and answer the following questions.

1. What is the number of the 7th flight listed on the chart?   Flight: #_____

   What time is the flight due to depart?   Time: _____

   What is the departure status of the flight?   Status: _____

   How long do you have to wait until the plane departs? Departure time: _____

   Present time: -_____

   Wait time: _____

2. What is the number of the 4th flight listed on the chart?   Flight: #_____

   What time is the flight due to depart?   Time: _____

   What is the departure status of the flight?   Status: _____

   How long do you have to wait until the plane departs? Departure time: _____

   Present time: -_____

   Wait time: _____

3. What is the number of the 10th flight listed on the chart?   Flight: #_____

   What time is the flight due to depart?   Time: _____

   What is the departure status of the flight?   Status: _____

   How long do you have to wait until the plane departs? Departure time: _____

   Present time: -_____

   Wait time: _____

C. Now, go to Gate 3 and watch the arrival of the next flight that comes to that gate. First, you must pass through the security check point. Name three things you see people put on the conveyer belt before they walk through the security gate. 1._____

   2._____   3._____

NAME:_____   DATE:_____

AIRPORT SIGNS - A

SIGN	WHERE DID YOU FIND IT?	COPY THE SIGN HERE
1. EXIT		
2. WOMEN		
3. MEN		
4. STOP		
5. PUSH		
6. PULL		
7. BUS		
8. TO GATES		

If you have extra time, find two more signs…

9.		
10.		

NAME: _____ DATE: _____

AIRPORT SIGNS - B

SIGN	WHAT DOES IT TELL YOU?	COPY THE SIGN HERE
1. CHECK IN		
2. TICKETING		
3. NO SMOKING		
4. PUBLIC PHONES		
5. ARRIVALS		
6. ENTRANCE		
7. SHORT TERM PARKING		
8. GIFTS		
9. SELF-SERVICE		
10. SMOKING AREA		
11. ELEVATOR		
12. LOWER LEVEL		
13. INFORMATION		
If you have extra time, find three more signs…		
14.		
15.		
16.		

NAME: _____ DATE:_____

Transporation

AIRPORT SIGNS - C

SIGN	WHAT DOES IT MEAN?	COPY THE SIGN HERE
1. BAGGAGE CLAIM		
2. UNITED AIR LINES		
3. HERTZ		
4. DEPARTURES		
5. CONCOURSE A		
6. AIRPORT SHUTTLE		
7. PARKING GARAGE		
8. INSURANCE		
9. COURTESY PHONE		
10. RESTAURANT		
11. AIRPORT TERMINAL		
12. RENTAL CAR RETURN		
13. TRAVELER'S AID		
14. GROUND TRANSPORTATION		
15. SECURITY CHECK		
If you have extra time, find three more signs…		
16.		
17.		
18.		

NAME: _____ DATE:_____

127 **Chapter Nine**

Restaurant Worksheets

Amount to Tip at a Restaurant

RESTAURANT

The shopping mall worksheets include fast food/food court eating options. A restaurant with individual menus and a serving staff is a significantly different experience. The restaurant worksheets address ordering from the menu, evaluating the service, paying the bill, and tipping the server.

Purpose:

Students will gain familiarity with a sit-down restaurant and learn to order, pay for their food, and tip their server.

Objectives:

Students will gain experience with:

1. Waiting and being seated in a restaurant.

2. Choosing foods from a menu and checking to be sure costs are manageable.

3. Giving a meal order to a server.

4. Paying for a meal.

5. Determining and including a tip for the server.

Academic Curriculum Connections:

Social Skills – Students must interact with the server and, perhaps, with a host or hostess. They will also be having a meal with classmates and perhaps some adults and will need to behave appropriately in the restaurant environment.

Mathematics – Students will estimate and calculate their bill by adding the costs of their menu items together, and they will calculate the tip using percentages. They will practice money skills, particularly counting change.

Health – Students will order from the menu, giving some consideration to food groups and balanced nutrition. They will also observe rules of cleanliness around food, such as washing their hands before eating.

Language Arts – Students will read the menu for information. They will also practice oral communication skills in obtaining information from the server and ordering their meals.

Preparation and Suggested Procedures:

Before a restaurant outing, the teacher may want to bring menus into the classroom and use them in conjunction with nutrition lessons. Students may also need considerable practice with concepts related to tipping and knowledge of the rationale for tipping. Teachers will need to be sure that all student meals can be paid for in some fashion so that students without money are not excluded from the activity.

Students will need to have money to pay for the meal (or arrangements will need to be made by the teacher). Also, if percentages present a difficult task for some students, they will want to take a tip guide with them. In order to make the restaurant experience transferable to the usual situation, it is suggested that students be seated at a number of small tables rather than all together in a group.

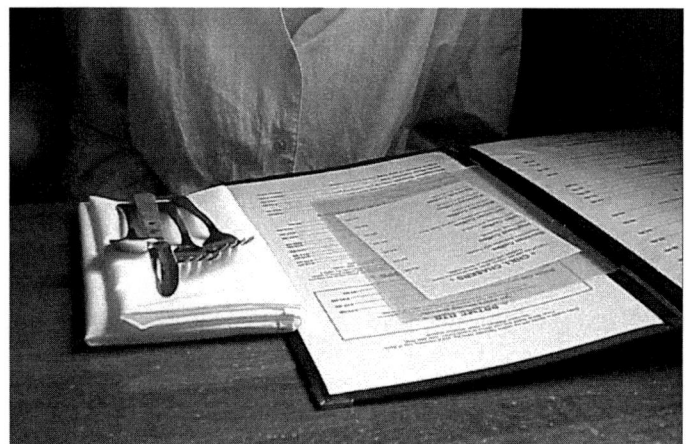

RESTAURANT WORKSHEET - A

READING THE MENU

1. What is the name of the restaurant? _____

2. Name something on the menu you would like to eat. _____

   How much does it cost? $_____. ___

ORDERING THE MEAL

1. Write down what you want to eat and tell the server. _____

   _____

   _____

TALKING WITH THE SERVER

Ask your server the following questions and write own the answers.

1. What is your name? _____

2. Where is the restroom?_____

3. Where do I pay the bill?_____

PAYING THE BILL

1. How much money do you owe for your meal? $_____. ___

2. How many dollar bills will you need to pay for your meal?_____

NAME: _____   DATE:_____

RESTAURANT WORKSHEET - B

READING THE MENU

1. How many different desserts are listed on your menu? _____

2. Pick three things on the menu you might like to order and tell how much each one costs.

Food Item	Cost
_____	$_____ . ___
_____	$_____ . ___
_____	$_____ . ___

3. Which one of the items you chose is the most expensive? _____

4. Which one of the items you chose is the least expensive?_____

ORDERING THE MEAL

1. Write down what you want to eat and give your order to the server.

Food Item	Cost
_____	$_____ . ___
_____	$_____ . ___
_____	$_____ . ___

2. What will your meal cost (without tax)?   Food total: $_____ . ___

   (add the cost of all the items together to get the food total)

RESTAURANT WORKSHEET - B (cont.)

TALKING WITH THE SERVER

Talk with your server and ask the following questions.

1. What kinds of soda pop do you have? _____

2. Are drink refills free?_____   If not, how much are they? $_____. ___

3. How many different salad dressings do you have?_____

   Write the name of the salad dressing you like best. _____

4. May I have the check please? Is the tax included?_____

PAYING THE BILL

1. Did you think the waiter did a good job?_____

   Why? _____

2. If you tip the waiter 15%, how much tip should you add to the bill?

   The cost of your meal including the tax: $_____. ___

   For the tip: X .15

   Amount of the tip: $_____. ___

3. How much money should you pay all together?

   The cost of your meal including the tax: $_____. ___

   Amount of the tip: +_____. ___

   Total you owe: $_____. ___

4. How many dollar bills will you need?_____

NAME: _____   DATE:_____

RESTAURANT WORKSHEET - C

READING THE MENU

1. How many different food sections are listed on your menu? _____

2. Name one food item listed under each section of the menu, list its main ingredient, and name the food group that the main ingredient comes from.

Menu Section	Food Item	Main Ingredient	Food Group
_____	_____	_____	_____
_____	_____	_____	_____
_____	_____	_____	_____
_____	_____	_____	_____
_____	_____	_____	_____

3. What is the most expensive entree on the menu and how much does it cost?

Food Item	Cost
_____	$_____ . ___

4. What is the least expensive appetizer on the menu and how much does it cost?

Food Item	Cost
_____	$_____ . ___

ORDERING THE MEAL

1. Write down what you want to eat and the cost of each item. Give your order to the server.

Food Item	Cost
_____	$_____ . ___
_____	$_____ . ___
_____	$_____ . ___

2. Now, estimate the cost of your meal with tax.

    (tax = tax rate X food total)

Food total: $_____ . ___

Plus tax: +_____ . ___

Total bill: $_____ . ___

RESTAURANT WORKSHEET - C (cont.)

TALKING WITH THE SERVER

While you are at the table, talk with your server and ask the following questions.

1. Do you have any daily specials?_____

   If so, what are they? _____

2. What side dishes are included with the meal I am ordering?_____

3. (Circle the server's answers for questions a. and b.)

   a. What days of the week is this restaurant open?

       Sunday   Monday   Tuesday   Wednesday   Thursday   Friday   Saturday

   b. What meals do you serve?   Breakfast   Lunch   Dinner

   c. When do you open and close each day? Open:_____ Close:_____

4. Do you deliver?_____ If so, do you have a carry out menu?_____
   May I have one to take with me, please?

PAYING THE BILL

1. What kind of service did you have?

   Check the one that best describes the service you received.

   _____ For **very good service** you will want to tip **20% (.20)**

   _____ For **good service** you should tip **15% (.15)**

   _____ For **poor service** you might tip only **10% (.10)**

   Now figure out the tip you should give the waiter.

         The cost of your meal including the tax: $_____.____

       The percentage that best describes the service you received: X _____.____

         Total you owe for your meal: $_____.____

2. If you only have a twenty dollar bill, how much change should you expect
   to get back after you pay your bill? $_____.____

NAME: _____ DATE:_____

AMOUNT TO TIP AT A RESTAURANT

Use this chart to decide the amount of tip you should leave on the table for your waiter when you are ready to pay your bill. Find the amount that is closest to the "total" on your bill in the left column, and then leave a tip that is equal to the amount of money listed in the right column.

10% TIP		15% TIP		20% TIP	
AMOUNT OF BILL	AMOUNT OF TIP	AMOUNT OF BILL	AMOUNT OF TIP	AMOUNT OF BILL	AMOUNT OF TIP
$ .65	$ .07	$ .65	$ .10	$ .65	$ .13
1.00	.10	1.00	.15	1.00	.20
1.35	.14	1.35	.21	1.35	.27
1.65	.17	1.65	.25	1.65	.33
2.00	.20	2.00	.30	2.00	.40
2.35	.24	2.35	.36	2.35	.47
2.65	.27	2.65	.40	2.65	.53
3.00	.30	3.00	.45	3.00	.60
4.00	.40	4.00	.60	4.00	.80
5.00	.50	5.00	.75	5.00	1.00
6.00	.60	6.00	.90	6.00	1.20
7.00	.70	7.00	1.05	7.00	1.40
8.00	.80	8.00	1.20	8.00	1.60
9.00	.90	9.00	1.35	9.00	1.80
10.00	1.00	10.00	1.50	10.00	2.00
12.00	1.20	12.00	1.80	12.00	2.40
15.00	1.50	15.00	2.25	15.00	3.00
17.00	1.70	17.00	2.55	17.00	3.40
20.00	2.00	20.00	3.00	20.00	4.00
25.00	2.50	25.00	3.75	25.00	5.00
30.00	3.00	30.00	4.50	30.00	6.00

Appendix

Picture Pages

Objectives and Evaluation

Discussion Questions

Overview of the G.A.I.N. Curriculum

Literature Related to the G.A.I.N. Curriculum

Reference List

PICTURE PAGES

The following series of pictures may be useful in helping students understand the sequence of events for particular activities as they prepare for excursions into the community. To illustrate, some students may want to use the pictures of ingredients in this section as a guide as they prepare to answer the questions on their recipe worksheet. Once the students return to the school after a trip into the community, picture pages may help students recall the various sights they saw or events that took place during their excursion. For example, the pictures of items such as magazines or CDs may help students decide what they want to check out when they return to the library. For those students who need additional cues, pictures can be assembled in a small booklet showing the sequence they should follow when they visit a specific community site.

Picture pages support the activities that have been described in many of the chapters in this book. Pictures are included as support for the materials in the following chapters:

Chapter One	–	Grocery Shopping
Chapter Two	–	Community Directions
Chapter Three	–	Mall
Chapter Four	–	Media
Chapter Five	–	Recipe Planning
Chapter Six	–	Hospital
Chapter Nine	–	Transportation
Chapter Ten	–	Restaurant

GROCERY STORE PICTURE PAGE

enter grocery store

check price

get basket or cart

check size

take out list

check brand or type

locate desired aisle

check date for freshness

find specific item

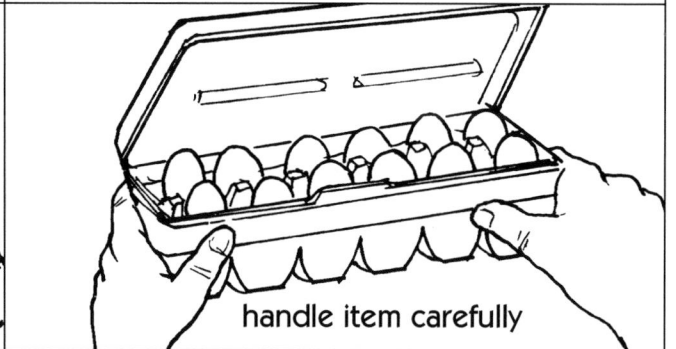

handle item carefully

GROCERY STORE PICTURE PAGE

arrange items in cart

go ahead as line moves

go on to next item

get money ready

select checkout lane

put items on counter

use express lanes

greet cashier and give coupons

go to the end of the line

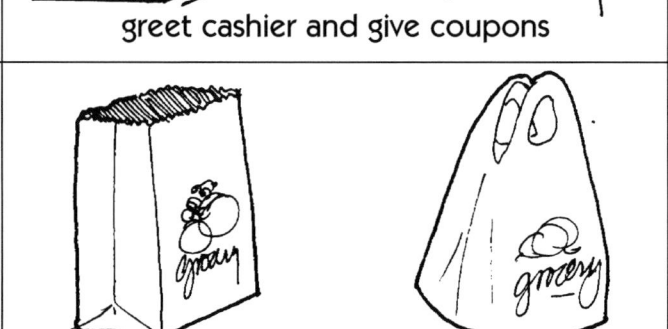

choose paper or plastic bags

GROCERY STORE PICTURE PAGE

pay cashier

get change

take bags and belongings

GROCERY DEPARTMENTS PICTURE PAGE

dairy

deli

produce

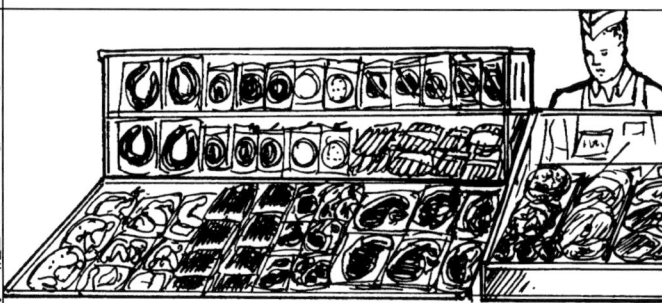

meat

bakery

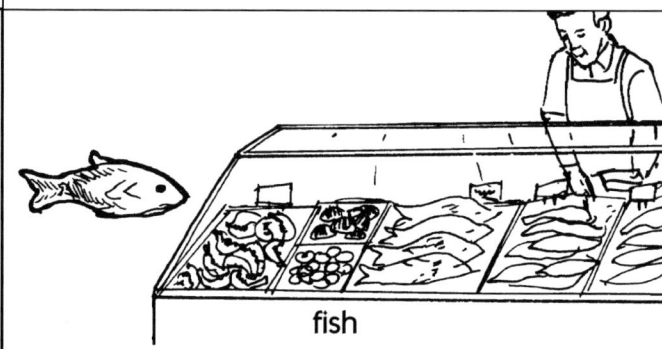

fish

frozen foods

GROCERY ITEMS PICTURE PAGE

beverages

cereal

cookies and crackers

canned fruits and vegetables

snack foods

soup

condiments

canned fish and meat

spices and herbs

rice and pasta

GROCERY ITEMS PICTURE PAGE

bread

ethnic foods

coffee and tea

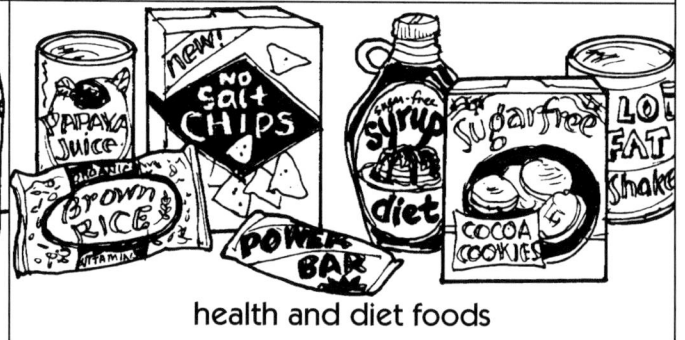

health and diet foods

liquor

baby products

candy

pet needs

baking supplies

paper products

GROCERY ITEMS PICTURE PAGE

laundry products

service desk

cleaning supplies

floral

personal products

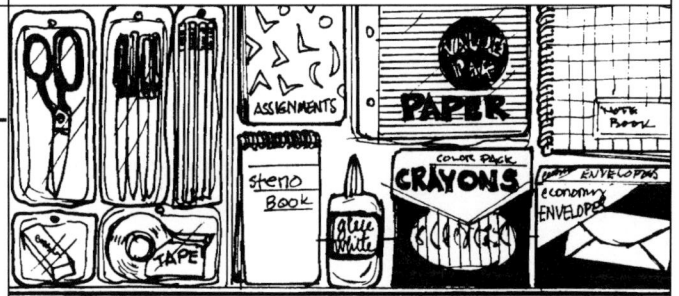
school and office supplies

health and beauty

video rental

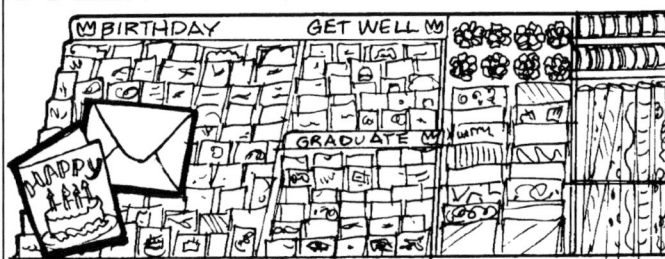
cards and gift wrap

paperbacks and magazines

GROCERY UNPACKING PICTURE PAGE

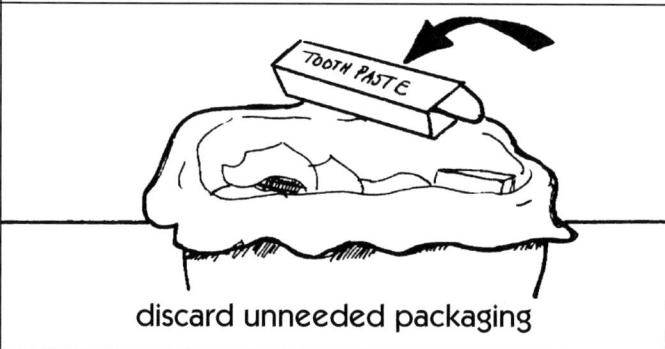

put bags on counter

put items under sink

empty bags

put other items away

put freezer items away

discard unneeded packaging

put refrigerated items away

put grocery bags away

put cupboard items away

refile shopping cards

INFORMATION SIGNS PICTURE PAGE

walk   pedestrian crossing

danger — keep out

don't walk

no trespassing

bus stop

do not enter

stop

watch your step

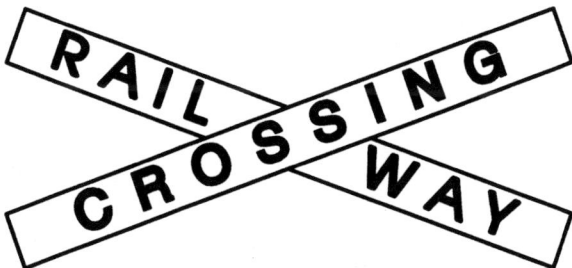

railroad crossing

beware of dog

BUILDING ACCESS SIGNS PICTURE PAGE

enter

do not enter

exit

wheelchair ramp

elevator

men's restroom

women's restroom

escalator

telephone

stairway

information

smoking

no smoking

FOOD COURT PICTURE PAGE

enter the restaurant

move ahead in line

enter correct restroom

prepare your order

wash your hands

greet cashier

go to counter

give coupons

select shortest line

order food

FOOD COURT PICTURE PAGE

show your order to the cashier

wait for food

eat here

to go

get condiments

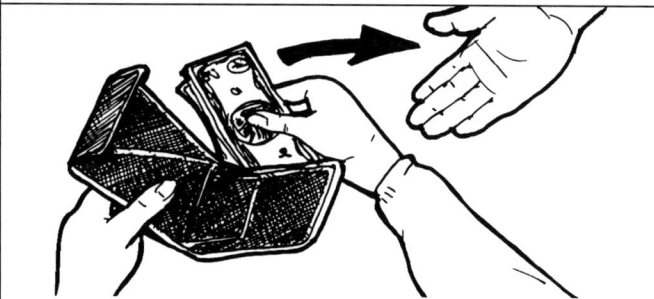

pay cashier

take napkins and straw

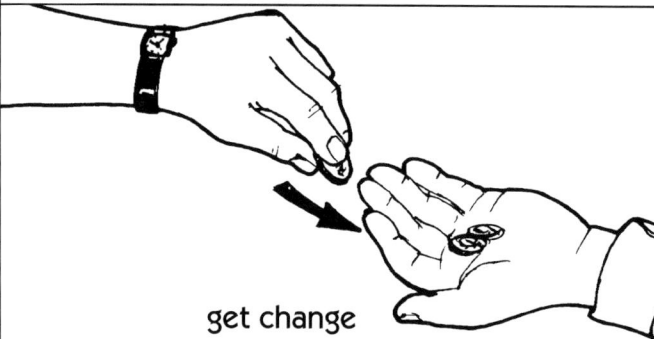

get change

get utensils

ask for condiments

choose clean table

FOOD COURT PICTURE PAGE

carry tray carefully

collect belongings

put tray on table

carry tray to counter

eat neatly

put trash in container

talk nicely

stack tray

clean table

exit restaurant

LIBRARY PICTURE PAGE

enter library

use computer (card catalog)

go to information desk if needed

locate material area

apply for library card

go to specific stack

TITLE

AUTHOR

know author's name and title if possible

follow call number and alphabetical order

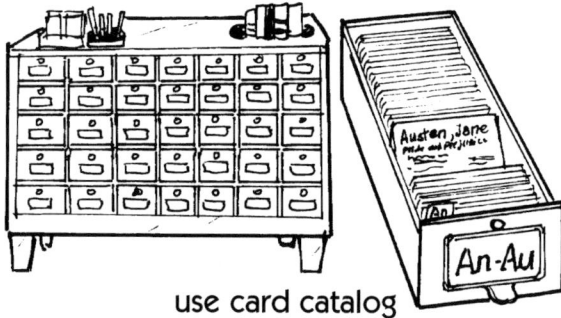

use card catalog

remove needed book from stack

LIBRARY PICTURE PAGE

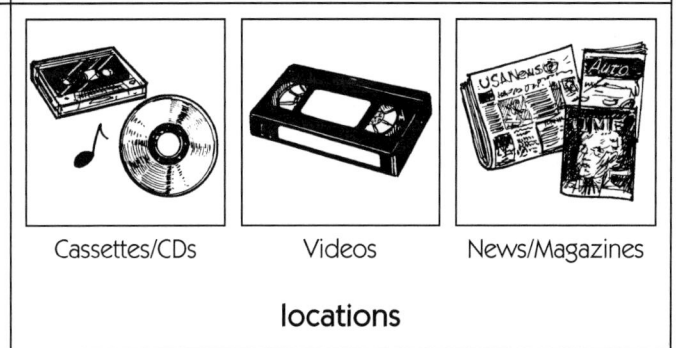

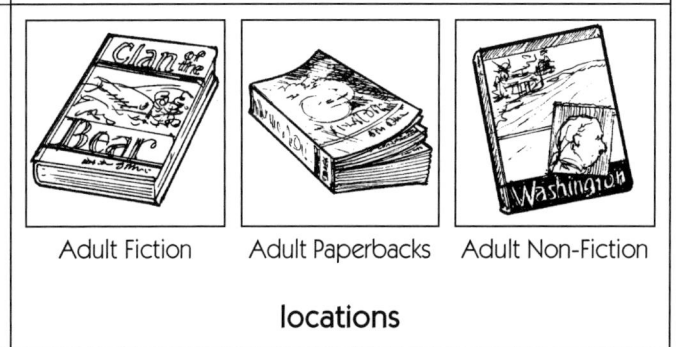

ask librarian for help

I'm looking for a biography of Bill Gates.

LATE!
pay fines

take materials to checkout counter

exit library with books and possessions

present library card

New

Large Print

Children/Youth

locations

take materials from librarian

Cassettes/CDs

Videos

News/Magazines

locations

RETURNS
October
DUE!
return items on due date

Adult Fiction

Adult Paperbacks

Adult Non-Fiction

locations

LIBRARY PICTURE PAGE

ask librarian for help

pay fines

take materials to checkout counter

exit library with books and possessions

present library card

New

Large Print

Children/Youth

locations

take materials from librarian

Cassettes/CDs

Videos

News/Magazines

locations

return items on due date

Adult Fiction

Adult Paperbacks

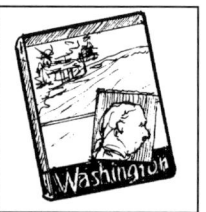

Adult Non-Fiction

locations

BREAKFAST PICTURE PAGE

Instant Oatmeal	instant oatmeal			
Oatmeal	oats			
Scrambled Eggs	eggs	milk		
Grits	quick grits	butter		
Bacon	bacon			
Sausage	breakfast sausage			
Burrito	eggs	tortillas	salsa	shredded cheese
Caramel Nut Rolls	8 refrigerator caramel rolls	chopped pecans		

SOUPS/BEVERAGES PICTURE PAGE

 **Hot Tea**	 tea bags		
 **Instant Coffee**	instant coffee		
 **Hot Chocolate**	cocoa mix	milk	
 **Hot Spiced Cider**	apple juice	cinnamon	
 **Cup-A-Soup**	Cup-A-Soup Mix		
 **Condensed Soup**	15 oz. condensed soup		
 **Vegetable Soup**	15 oz. Italian style chicken broth	15 oz. tomato pieces	 frozen soup vegetables

MAIN DISHES PICTURE PAGE

Beef Stew 	 24 oz. beef stew				
Canned Ravioli 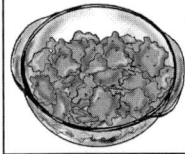	15 oz. can ravioli				
Pot Pie	frozen pot pie				
Hot Dogs 	 hot dogs	hot dog buns			
Pork Chops 	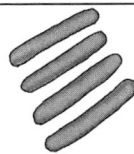 1 lb. boneless pork chops	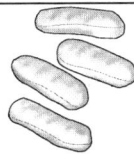 mustard			
Baked Ham 	 1 ½ lb. canned ham	8 oz. pineapple chunks			
Beans & Wieners 	wieners	15 oz. baked beans			
Meatloaf 	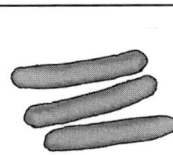 1 ½ lb. ground beef	8 oz. tomato juice or V8	oats	eggs	onion
Sloppy Joes 	 1 ½ lb. lean ground beef	sloppy joe mix	6 oz. tomato paste	hamburger buns	

MAIN DISHES PICTURE PAGE

 **Meatballs**	 1 ½ lb. ground beef	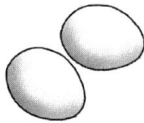 eggs	onion	Italian style bread crumbs	garlic powder
 **Macaroni Casserole**	 1 ½ lb. ground beef	26 oz. spaghetti sauce	8 oz. tomato sauce	elbow macaroni	shredded cheese
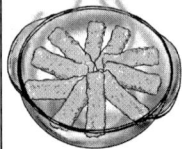 **Fish Sticks**	 frozen fish sticks	lemon juice			
 **Fish Filets**	 1 lb. fish filets	Italian style bread crumbs			
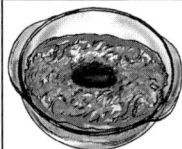 **Tuna Ring**	eggs	12 oz. can tuna	 bread crumbs	celery	onion	green pepper
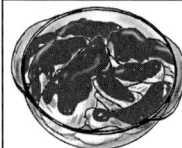 **Barbecue Chicken**	 3 lb. chicken pieces	barbecue sauce			
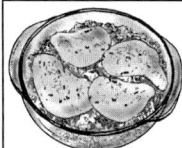 **Chicken Casserole**	 4 skinless, boneless chicken breasts	rice	 fresh broccoli	10 ¾ oz. mushroom soup	paprika
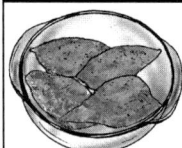 **Shake'n Bake Chicken**	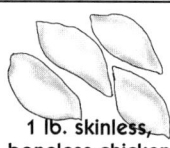 1 lb. skinless, boneless chicken breasts	Shake 'n Bake for chicken			
 **Pot Roast**	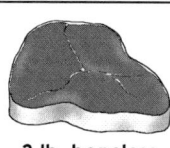 3 lb. boneless chuck roast	onion soup mix			

SIDE DISHES PICTURE PAGE

Rice	rice	butter	
Rice-A-Roni	Rice-A-Roni	butter	
Spanish Rice	rice	butter	thick and chunky salsa
Baked Beans	16 oz. pork and beans	mustard	brown sugar
Baked Potatoes	baking potatoes		
Sweet Potatoes	sweet potatoes		
Instant Potatoes	potato flakes	milk	
Gravy	gravy mix		
Parsley Potatoes	potatoes	butter	parsley flakes

SIDE DISHES PICTURE PAGE

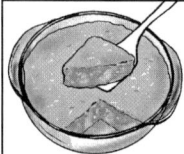 Corn Bread	egg	8 1/2 oz. corn muffin mix	milk	PAM	
 Stove Top Stuffing	Stove Top stuffing	butter			
 Beans and Rice	11 oz. V8	15 oz. pinto beans	11 oz. can corn	rice	thick and chunky salsa

VEGETABLES PICTURE PAGE

 Green Beans	14 oz. can green beans
 Canned Peas	14 oz. can peas
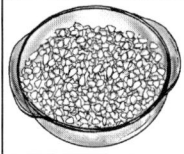 Canned Corn	14 oz. can corn
 Canned Greens	14 oz. can greens or kale
 Canned Carrots	14 oz. can sliced carrots

VEGETABLES PICTURE PAGE

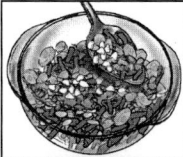

Mixed Vegetables	10 oz. frozen mixed vegetables
Frozen Peas	10 oz. frozen peas
Baby Carrots	1 lb. bag fresh baby carrots
Broccoli	1 lb. fresh broccoli
Acorn Squash	1 lb. acorn squash
Corn on the Cob	3 ears corn

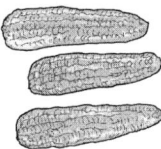

DESSERTS PICTURE PAGE

 **Baked Apples**	 4 apples	sugar	cinnamon		
 **Chinese Cookies**	 6 oz. chocolate chips	6 oz. butterscotch chips	3 oz. can chow mein noodles	salted peanuts	
 **Jello**	 small package jello				
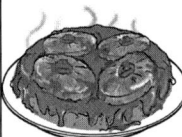 **Pineapple Cake**	Jiffy yellow cake mix	brown sugar	eggs	butter	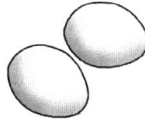 8 oz. can pineapple	PAM
 **Brownies**	flour	milk	eggs	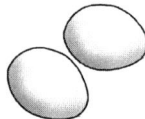 sugar	 unsweetened cocoa
	butter	PAM	vanilla	baking powder	
 **S'Mores**	 marshmallows	graham crackers	 chocolate candy bar		

MEDICAL PROCEDURES PICTURE PAGE

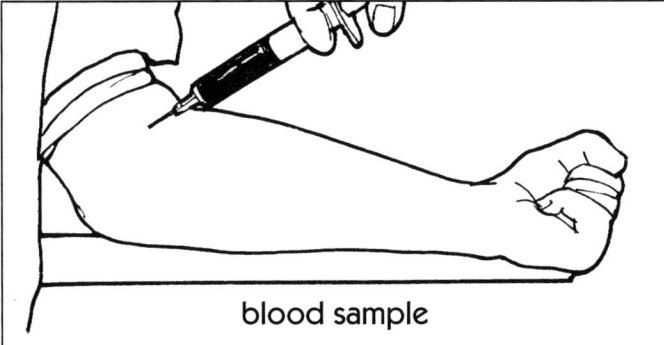

blood sample

x-ray

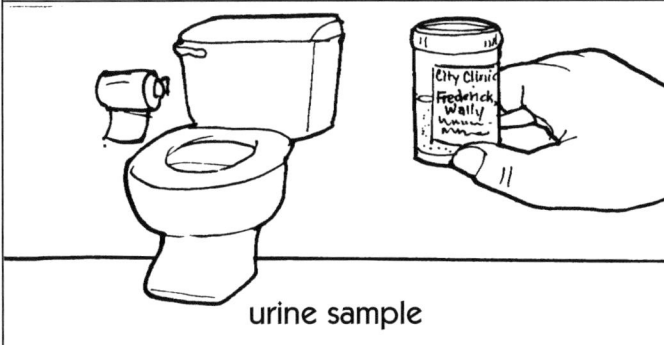

urine sample

prescription

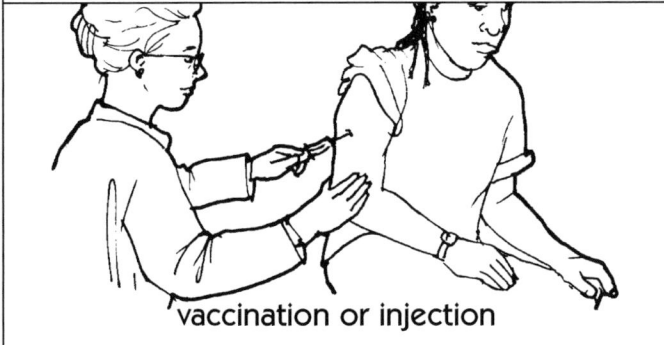

vaccination or injection

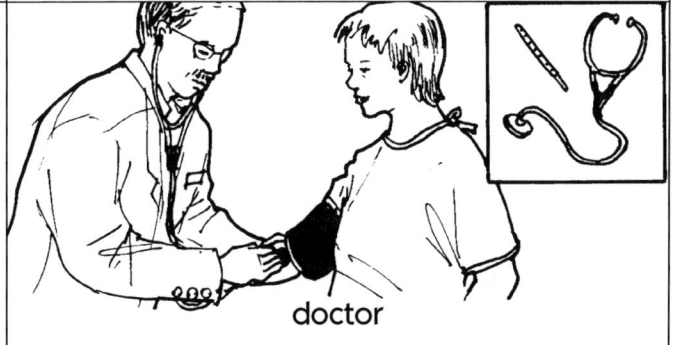

doctor

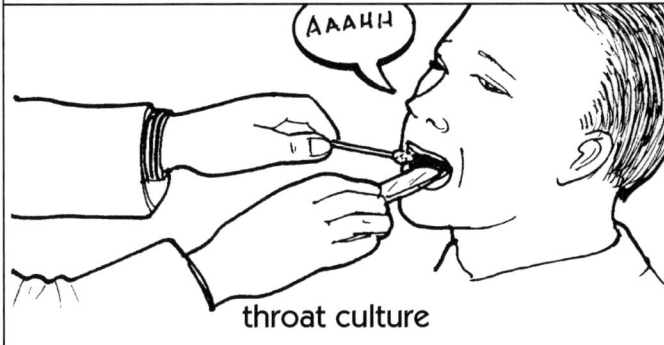

throat culture

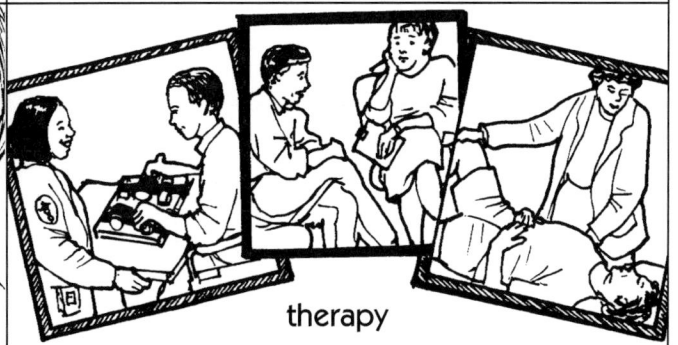

therapy

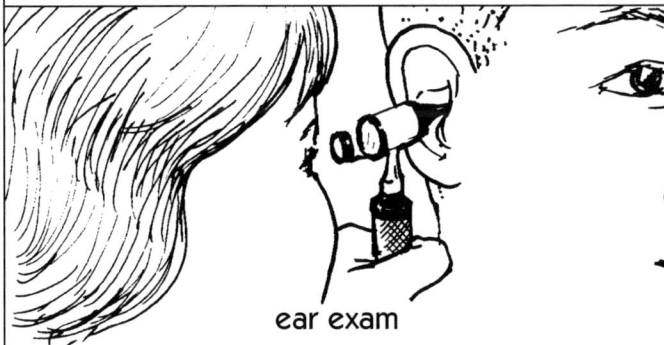

ear exam

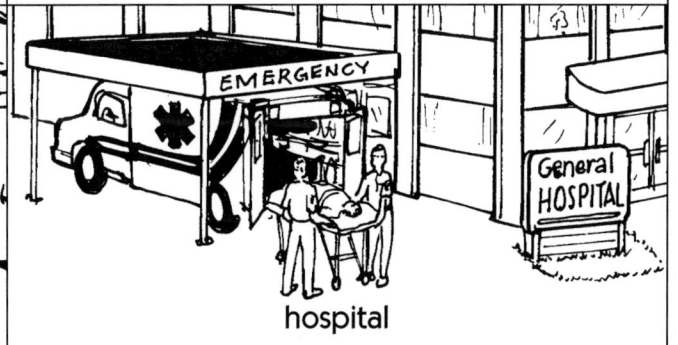

hospital

MEDICAL SPECIALTIES PICTURE PAGE

family practice

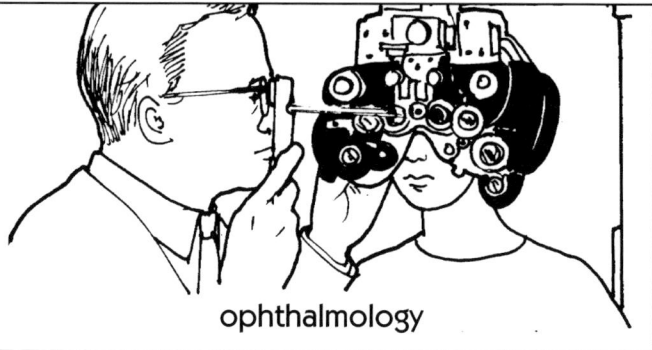

ophthalmology

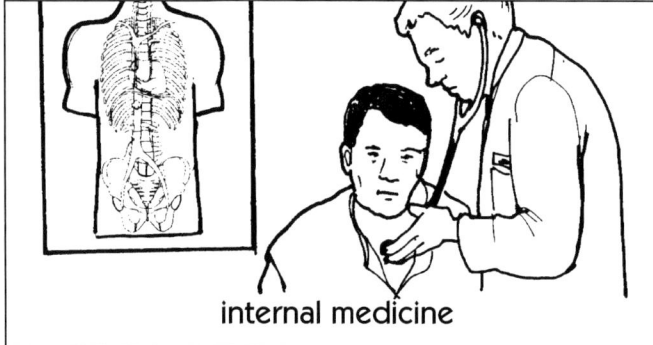

internal medicine

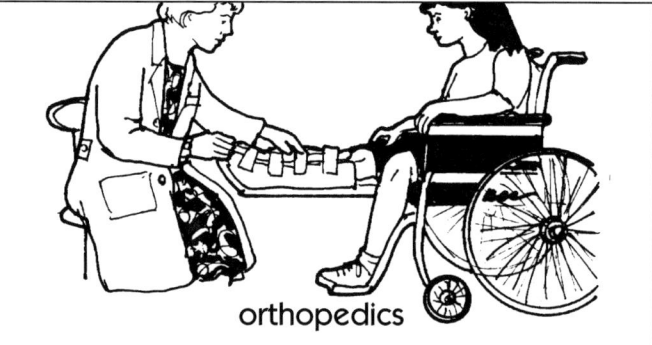

orthopedics

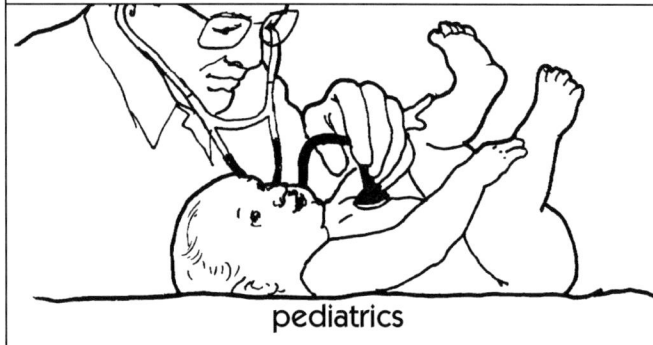

pediatrics

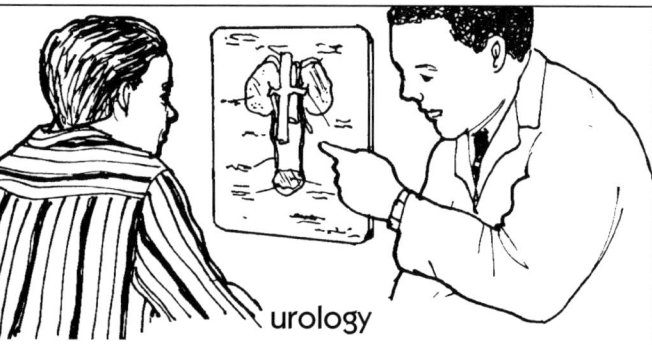

urology

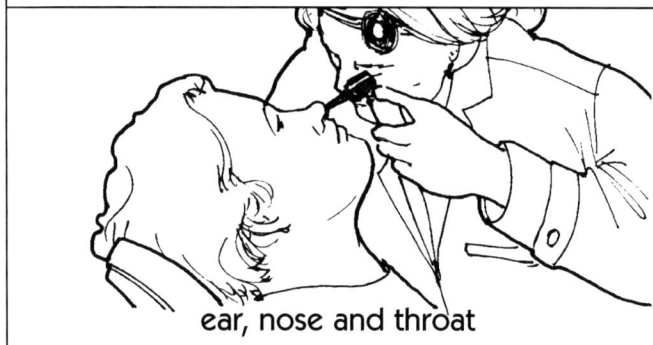

ear, nose and throat

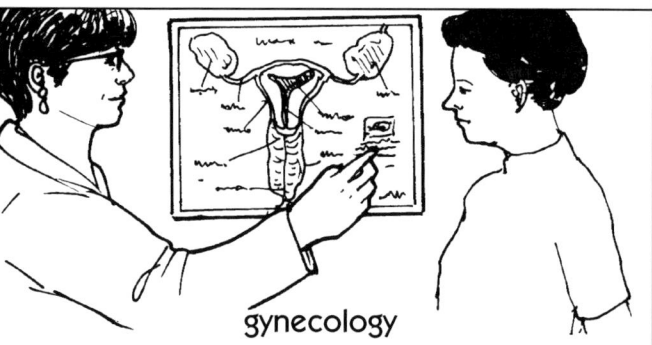

gynecology

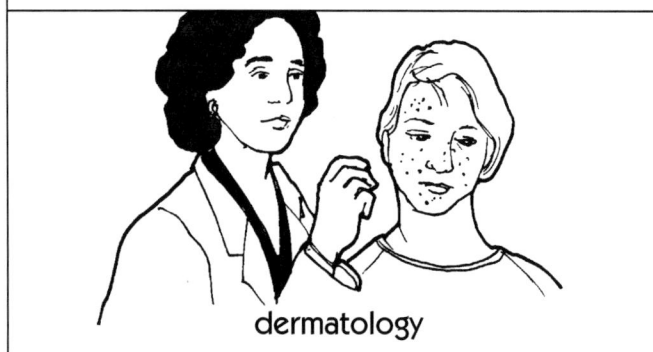

dermatology

psychology/psychiatry

AIRPLANE PICTURE PAGE

gather your luggage and ticket

select bags to check

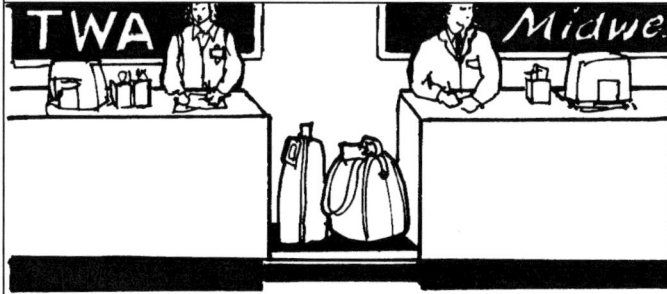

locate check-in for baggage

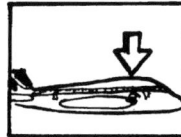

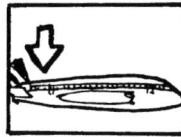

request seat assignment

locate airline counter

put ticket and boarding pass in safe place

wait in line

GATES 15-20

GATES 1-7

GATES 8-14

find departure gate

present ticket and I.D.

place bags on conveyer

AIRPLANE PICTURE PAGE

walk through detector and pick up your bag

find your assigned seat

proceed to gate

stow bags

wait until your flight is called

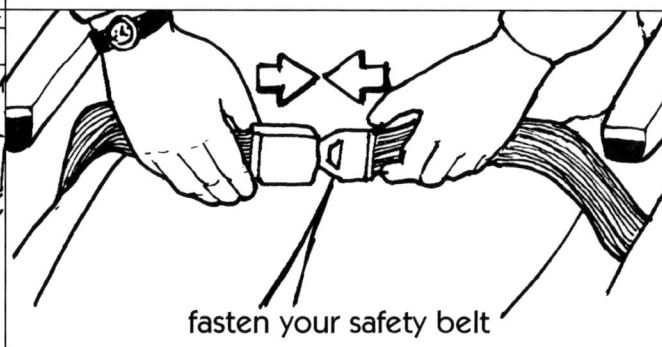

fasten your safety belt

get in boarding line

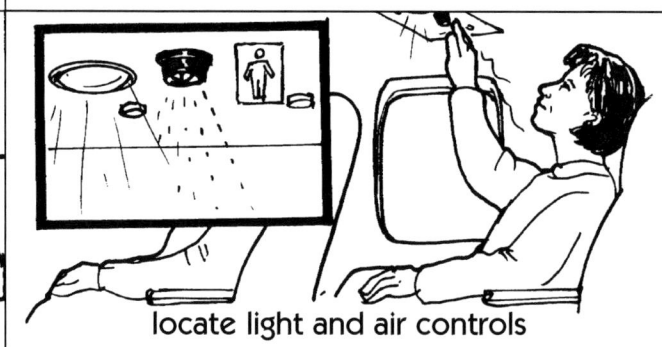

locate light and air controls

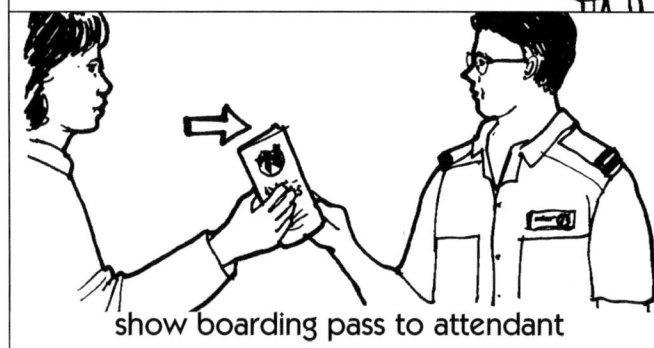

show boarding pass to attendant

ask for help if needed

AIRPLANE PICTURE PAGE

occupy your time

collect belongings

food and beverage is served

exit as aisle clears

find bathroom(s)

exit plane

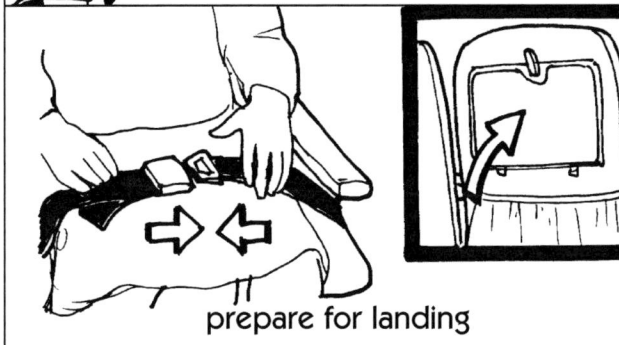
prepare for landing

collect your baggage

stay seated until notified

exit airline terminal

TRANSPORTATION MATCHING

Draw a line from the picture to the matching word.

   train

   car

   truck

   subway

   airplane

   bus

   bike

   taxi

   motorcycle

   ship

Draw a line from the word to the matching picture.

wheelchair

bike

ship

taxi

truck

train

bus

car

subway

airplane

TRANSPORTATION MATCHING

Write the letter from the picture next to the matching word.

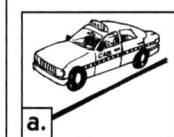 a.

_____ bus

 b.

_____ subway

 c.

_____ ship

 d.

_____ taxi

 e.

_____ truck

 a.

_____ train

 b.

_____ wheelchair

 c.

_____ car

 d.

_____ bike

 e.

_____ motorcycle

Write the word for the picture. Choose from the list on the right.

_____

_____

_____

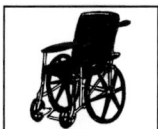

_____

_____

motorcycle

wheelchair

train

bike

car

_____

_____

_____

_____

_____

subway

airplane

truck

taxi

ship

TRANSPORTATION MATCHING

Cross out the pictures/words that do not belong.

 bike	 wheelchair	 taxi	 airplane	 party	 train
 truck	 subway	 bus	 tiger	 washing machine	 motorcycle
 bathtub	 stove	 ship	 rocking chair	 airplane	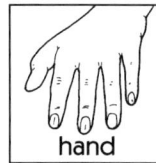 hand
 car	 typewriter	 subway	 transportation	 bus	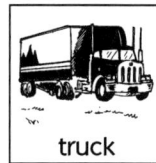 truck

Circle the word that matches.

ship	shirt	ship	sink	suit	sheep
airplane	appetizer	ambulance	airport	airplane	arrive
train	tennis	truck	train	tired	today
bike	baker	bear	big	bike	bird
wheelchair	Walgreens	wheelchair	waitress	woman	weak
motorcycle	microwave	mechanic	mountain	motorcycle	mother
bus	bowl	bed	butter	boy	bus
subway	sweater	summer	Safeway	subway	surfing
car	cat	cards	car	class	cave
truck	tractor	train	truck	try	tree

CAR PICTURE PAGE

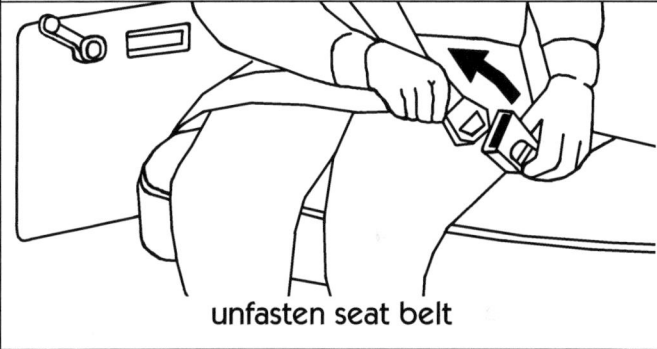

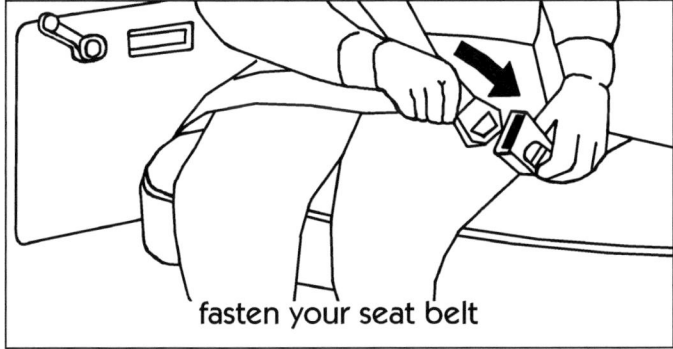

choose where to sit

lock your door

open the door

ask before adjusting

sit in the car

unfasten seat belt

close the door, watch for fingers

open the door and get out

fasten your seat belt

close the door, watch for fingers

TABLE SERVICE PICTURE PAGE

enter restaurant

a table for _____, please

check coat

hang coat

table

booth

counter

greet host

follow host to table

wait to be seated

say thank you!

no smoking, please

look at menu

TABLE SERVICE PICTURE PAGE

greet server

go to salad bar

ask for separate bills

take condiments or crackers

order beverage

thank server

order food

use correct restroom

wait patiently

order dessert

TABLE SERVICE PICTURE PAGE

eat neatly

pay server

wait for change

talk nicely

pay cashier

wait for change

ask for service

collect belongings

review bill

get coat

leave tip

exit restaurant

OBJECTIVES AND EVALUATION

1. By _____, when on a school trip, student will initiate a conversation with an adult member of the community _____ time(s).

2. By _____, when on a school trip, student will effectively (independently/with teacher prompts) ask for help from a member of the community or store employee _____ time(s).

3. By _____, when on a school trip and asked a question by a member of the community or store employee, student will answer the question appropriately _____ % of the time.

4. By _____, when on a school trip, student will (make eye contact/stand at an appropriate distance to respect the personal space of others) when interacting with a member of the community or store employee _____ % of the time.

5. By _____ , when on a school trip, student will interact appropriately with (adults/peers) without becoming disruptive _____ % of the time.

6. By _____, when on a school trip, student will refrain from touching/picking up store items that s/he is not going to purchase _____ % of the time.

7. By _____, student will complete an assigned worksheet without being distracted _____ % of the time.

8. By _____, when experiencing difficulty completing a worksheet, student will seek help from (a peer/the teacher/a community member/store employee) _____ % of the time.

9. By _____, student will demonstrate the use of appropriate (greeting/honorific/manners/voice level/language) when talking with a community member or store employee _____ % of the time.

10. By _____, when participating in group activities, student will work collaboratively with his/her classmates (to allow all members of the group to participate/to complete assigned share of duties) _____ % of the time.

11. By _____, student will be dressed appropriately during activities in the (community/school) _____ % of the time.

12. By _____, student will be ready on time when (going to/leaving) activities in the (community/school) _____ % of the time.

DISCUSSION QUESTIONS

You can extend the activities in this book and further encourage student independence by asking your students to think more critically and to solve any problems they encounter as they participate in their community. The following questions, or similar questions that you create, will support your students in becoming self-directed and proactive adults.

Use the following questions to encourage student interaction during a community excursion:

1. (When a student plans to engage in a social interaction/conversation with a member of the community or store employee, help him/her prepare.)

   a. With whom do you think it will be all right to have a conversation?

   b. Why do you want to talk to _____?

   c. How will you start your interaction with _____?

   d. How can your interaction with _____ be beneficial?

   e. With whom do you think you should avoid interacting? Why?

2. (Instead of providing the help needed when a student does not know the answer to one of the questions on his/her worksheet, have the student ask the most appropriate community member or store employee.)

   a. Who do you think you should ask for help?

   b. Why do you think _____ is the best person to help you?

   c. What should you say to that person?

   d. What do you think you will learn from _____?

3. (After the student has had a social interaction with/elicited help from the community member or store employee, ask follow-up questions.)

   a. Who did you talk to?

   b. Did you enjoy talking to _____? Why/why not?

   c. Who initiated the interaction/conversation?

d. What did you talk about?

e. What did you learn from _____?

f. How can that information help you?

g. How will you use that information?

Use the following questions for a student discussion as the culminating activity to extend/complement community related experiences:

1. (After the student has returned to school following a trip into the community, ask follow-up questions.)

   a. During our trip to _____, did you talk with anyone other than the people in our group?

   b. Who did you talk to?

   c. What was (his/her) job/role in the community?

   d. What did you ask (him/her)?

   e. What did (s/he) say to you?

   f. How will you know who you should talk to and who you should avoid the next time you need help?

2. (The following questions may be helpful in the classroom either after the student has returned to school following a trip into the community or to enhance discussions related to classroom activities. Use these questions for either circumstance.)

   a. How can you use the information you learned?

   b. What will you do the next time you need help?

   c. Why is it important sometimes to ask for help?

   d. What are some things you should try to do before you ask someone to help you?

OVERVIEW OF THE G.A.I.N CURRICULUM

Philosophy and Purpose

The purpose of the G.A.I.N. program is to give students the skills and self-confidence necessary to facilitate their integration into the community. This integration begins in the classroom community and the community of the school, but its most important function is to ease students into the broader community beyond the school. Because social skills are a key to successful integration, the classroom and community activities in the G.A.I.N. curriculum are designed to enhance social skills as well as to develop functional skills for independent living. As students gain competence, they become more confident. Developing the self-esteem of students is another primary goal of the activities.

Classroom structure and the functional curriculum itself foster individual development within a context of group cohesion. Many activities involve group interaction and interdependence. Even when students are working individually on materials that are appropriate to their own learning, all other students in the room are doing similar work. Since the demands and expectations for all students are generally the same, they have a better sense of the continuity of their work, are able to answer each other's questions, and feel less isolated and more part of the classroom group.

A student's self-confidence and self-esteem are enhanced when he or she becomes an accepted member of a group and experiences success. Students in the G.A.I.N. program are asked to do work appropriate to their skill levels, guaranteeing that they will experience success. They learn to evaluate their work and monitor their progress. Development of social skills is promoted in much the same way. Students are encouraged to take responsibility for themselves and to be as independent as they can be. They are helped to become successful in their interactions with each other and then learn to generalize their skills to interactions with other peers, with people in positions of authority, and with people in service positions. Generalization of skills is not assumed, but is fostered by experiences in the community that are an integral part of the curriculum.

Description of the G.A.I.N. Curriculum

An overview of the entire G.A.I.N. curriculum—not just the aspects of it that appear in this G.A.I.N. book—may help to clarify its functional focus and its methods of achieving the goals described above.

Although the curriculum is holistic in the sense that all activities are geared toward integration into the community and successful transition to adulthood, some activities are specifically suited for integration into the classroom or the school. Therefore, for organizational purposes, aspects of the curriculum will be categorized according to the level of community specifically addressed.

Integration into the Community of the Classroom

The complete G.A.I.N. curriculum uses activities designed to encourage all individuals to develop competence and confidence in the relatively safe environment of the classroom. The entire class plays academic and life-skills games together, even though each participant is working on his or her own IEP objectives and materials while playing. Weekly round-table discussions on topics relevant to the students' lives include all class members and stress respect for each individual and for all opinions expressed. "Social time" once each week requires each student to interact with at least one peer in the group. A breakfast restaurant for school staff and students, a yearly gift-wrapping project, and periodic car washes foster group cooperation and interdependence while each student performs a job at his or her own skill level.

All students work on work boxes, at the same time, such as those described in Work Boxes (Hamill & Dunlevy, 1999). They take responsibility for getting the materials, reading the instructions, requesting help if necessary, and completing their work as independently as possible. They have a sense of what everyone else is doing and why. A shared sense of purpose contributes to the group feeling in the classroom.

Integration into the Community of the School

Students are integrated into the school community through classroom inclusion as appropriate; through work-study positions in the library and cafeteria and in janitorial services; and through fundraising projects that involve the staff and students of the school. The major integrating activity, other than inclusion in the general education classroom and work-study positions, is a carry-out breakfast restaurant. Students and teachers come to the restaurant, which is located in the classroom. They must interact with special education students to place and obtain orders and to pay and receive change. Students from the class also record, fill, and deliver orders from customers throughout the building.

Integration into the Community Beyond the School

Since integration into the broader community is the primary long-term goal of the G.A.I.N. program, most activities, even those mentioned for classroom and school integration, ultimately facilitate integration into the broader community. These activities are as "real" as possible to maximize generalization of learned skills to the settings requiring them in daily life. Classroom activities specifically targeting community integration include reading classified ads and completing job applications.

As illustrated in this book, community-based learning other than vocational preparation is also part of the curriculum, easing the transition from school to the community. Students go to work sites in the community (or in the school if they are not yet prepared for community sites) for two hours twice each week. The school provides supervision as students do real work for minimum wages. Additional outings into the community are planned approximately once a week so that students may practice consumer skills (comparative shopping, using coupons, and shopping sales); enjoy leisure time pursuits (bowling, hiking, going to the zoo, and eating out); learn to read maps and signs in order to increase their independence; and become familiar with community services, such as the hospital.

LITERATURE RELATED TO THE G.A.I.N. CURRICULUM

The activities in the G.A.I.N. program are classroom tested. The functional and group approaches have been expanded because they have been productive. They also reflect much current thinking regarding needs and emphases in special education.

Functional Curriculum

The growing demand for inclusive classrooms has encouraged renewed scrutiny of curriculum. Inclusion advocates frequently suggest functional and/or community-based learning as effective methods to use in inclusive classrooms. Definitions of "functional" for inclusive and/or special education vary somewhat. The definition offered by Clark (1994) is representative and corresponds well with the G.A.I.N. program's functional emphasis:

> A functional curriculum approach is a way of delivering instructional content that focuses on the concepts and skills needed by all students with disabilities in the areas of personal-social, daily living, and occupational adjustment. What is considered a functional curriculum for any one student would be the content (concepts and skills) included in that student's curriculum or course of study that targets his or her current and future needs. These needs are based on a nondiscriminatory, functional assessment approach. (Clark, 1994, p. 37)

Dever and Knapczyk's view is similar:

> In functional instruction, the content of instruction consists of the skills people normally need to live out their lives in the community. It often takes place in the community setting in which people normally interact and can be delivered in a variety of forms, including on-the-job vocational training, service learning, applied academics, and others. (Dever and Knapczyk, 1997, pp. 16-17)

Peterson, LeRoy, Field, and Wood (1992), in recommending changes in curriculum content, state that "students should learn to perform meaningful activities in areas that are important to their daily lives and apply skills they learn in math, science, language, and other areas." (Peterson et al., 1992, p. 210) The G.A.I.N. program refers to this experiential, applied way of learning academic subject matter as "applied academics," one major component of a functional curriculum.

The G.A.I.N. program has much in common with the features of career education described by Brolin (1989). He indicates that career education is a process of integrating new concepts, materials, and experiences into traditional subject matter, without replacing it. He believes that students with developmental disabilities benefit from experiential learning. "If students are busily engaged in something they like, and if it has a meaningful goal related to their future lives, motivation will increase and behavior problems will diminish." (Brolin, 1989, pp. 2-3) A focus on functional skills does not detract from academic learning; rather, it can increase learning and promote career development as well (Brolin & Gysbers, 1989, p. 158).

Special education teachers recognize the value of teaching functional skills, but many apparently feel that they lack the background necessary to teach them. Survey results reported by Halpern (1985) and by Sands, Adams, and Stout (1995) suggest that teachers want training to improve their skills in functional areas of the curriculum.

Community-Based Learning

Community-based learning is endorsed by increasing numbers of special educators and advocates of inclusion. Peterson, LeRoy, Field, and Wood (1992) conclude that "curriculum for all students should be radically restructured so that it is community-referenced in both content and process of learning." (Peterson et al., 1992, p. 209).

Udvari-Solner and Thousand (1995) state a similar opinion:

> Given the complexities of adult life in the 21st Century, educators are realizing that all the skills that are relevant, critical, and enriching cannot be taught effectively within the confines of the classroom. For students with significant disabilities who may experience problems generalizing skills acquired in one setting to another, the need for systematic instruction in the actual environment of concern is evident. (Udvari-Solner & Thousand, p. 94)

Other authors who stress the importance of community-based learning include: Falvey (1989); Wehman and Revell (1997); Beck, Broers, Hogue, Shipstead, and Knowlton (1994); Wiggins and Behrmann (1989); McDonnell and Hardman (1985); Mithaug, Martin, and Agran (1987); and Artesani and Itkonen (1995).

Group Instruction

The G.A.I.N. program uses primarily group instruction rather than individual instruction. Brolin believes that a cooperative learning and teaching environment is needed in special education and indicates that it can be more effective than either a competitive or individualistic environment (1989, p. 4). Other authors also address the use of small group instruction rather than individual instruction for maximum effectiveness. Stinson, Gast, Wolery, and Collins (1991) found that group instruction can not only be more efficient but can also provide opportunities for modeling and observational learning to occur. They showed that students with developmental disabilities can be taught individually within a group, and that these students do learn through observation in that situation. Stainback, Stainback, and Slavin acknowledge that individual work may be necessary in some situations but indicate that "in general, properly organized group activities can be highly effective in meeting students' unique, personalized learning goals." (Stainback, Stainback, and Slavin, 1989, p. 137)

The G.A.I.N. program employs instructional games as one preferred way of teaching individuals in a group context. The use of educational games in small groups has not been addressed frequently in the literature. Beattie and Algozzine (1982) compared the effectiveness of games and worksheets for arithmetic teaching. Using a test of the material presented and an observational measure of time on task, they found that the game format was more effective (Beattie and Algozzine, p. 257): "Specifically, games provide practice accompanied by immediate feedback and motivational cues (e.g., 'pay attention or you lose your turn'). They also enable students to 'socialize' while doing work." (Beattie and Algozzine, p. 256) Blum and Yacom (1996) talk about the benefits of instructional games for student learning. They point out that games are naturally motivating and fun, that games facilitate individualization of instruction and assessment, that games help make abstract concepts more concrete, and that games allow students to learn from each other and build self-esteem (Blum and Yacom, pp. 60, 61).

Leveling of Materials

Concepts similar to the G.A.I.N. program's leveling of materials are referred to in some of the literature dealing with curriculum adaptations for inclusive classrooms. In describing a "community integration program" in a Virginia school, Wiggins and Behramann (1989) mention employing different objectives for students at different levels of functioning while they are all participating in the same activity together (Wiggins and Behrmann, p. 23). Both Falvey (1996) and York, Doyle, and Kronberg (1992) refer to "multi-level instruction" when students participate in the same activities but with different levels of difficulty or with different objectives. Falvey's concept is broader than leveling in the G.A.I.N. program but includes teaching the same curriculum at different degrees of complexity, teaching the same curriculum but with functional or direct application to daily life, and teaching the same curriculum but with varying performance standards, all of which adaptations are sometimes used in G.A.I.N. leveling. "Overlapping curriculum" is another concept that captures some of the characteristics of leveling (Van Dyke et al., p. 478 and York et al., p. 13).

Conclusion

While many sources stress the importance of functional and social skills, community-based learning, transitional skills, and self-esteem, fewer sources talk about the specifics of how to incorporate these features into the curriculum, particularly for students at different levels of ability. The materials in this book attempt to fill this gap by providing specific, concrete classroom materials and instructions for their use so that special education teachers can implement this approach in their classrooms.

REFERENCE LIST

Artesani, A. J., Itkonen, T., Fryxell, D., and Woolcock, W. W. "Community Instruction," *Instructional Strategies in the Community: A Resource Guide for Community Instruction for Persons with Disabilities,*. W. W. Woolcock and J. W. Domarack, eds., Austin, TX: Pro-Ed, Inc., 1995.

Beattie, J., and Algozzine, B. "Improving Basic Academic Skills of Educable Mentally Retarded Adolescents." *Education and Training of the Mentally Retarded,* 1982, vol. 17, pp. 255-258.

Beck, J., Broers, J., Hogue, E., Shipstead, J., and Knowlton, E., "Strategies for Functional Community-based Instruction and Inclusion for Children with Mental Retardation," *Teaching Exceptional Children,* 1994, vol. 26, pp. 44-48.

Blum, H. T. and Yacom, D. J. "A Fun Alternative: Using Instructional Games to Foster Student Learning," *Teaching Exceptional Children,* 1996, vol. 29, pp. 60-63.

Brigance, A.H. *Brigance Comprehensive Inventory of Basic Skills,* North Billerica, MA: Curriculum Associates, Inc., 1983.

Brigance, A. H., *Brigance Diagnostic Inventory of Essential Skills,* North Billerica, MA: Curriculum Associates, Inc., 1981.

Brolin, D. E., ed. *Life-Centered Career Education: A Competency-Based Approach,* Reston, VA: The Council for Exceptional Children, 1989.

Brolin, D. E., and Gysbers, N. C. "Career Education for Students with Disabilities." *Journal of Counseling and Development,* 1989, vol. 68, pp. 155-159.

Clark, G. M., "Is a Functional Curriculum Approach Compatible with an Inclusive Education Model?" *Teaching Exceptional Children,* 1994, vol. 26, pp. 36-39.

Dever, R. B. and Knapczyk, D. R., *Teaching Persons with Mental Retardation: A Model for Curriculum Development and Teaching,* Chicago: Brown and Benchmark Publishers, 1997.

Falvey, M. A., *Community-based Curriculum: Instructional Strategies for Students with Severe Handicaps (2nd ed.),* Baltimore: Paul H. Brookes Publishing Co., 1989.

Falvey, M. A., Ginner, C. C., and Kimm, C., "What Do I Do Monday Morning?" *Inclusion: A Guide for Educators.* S. Stainback and W. Stainback, eds. Baltimore: Paul H. Brookes Publishing Co., 1996.

Halpern, A.S., "Transition: A Look at the Foundations," *Exceptional Children,* 1985, vol. 51, pp. 479-486.

Hamill, L. and Dunlevy, A., *Work Boxes*, San Antonio TX: PCI Educational Publishing, 1999.

McDonnell, J. and Hardman, M., "Planning the Transition of Severely Handicapped Youth from School to Adult Services: A Framework for High School Programs." *Education and Training of the Mentally Retarded,* 1985, vol. 20, pp. 275-286.

Mithaug, D., Martin, J. E., and Agran, M., "Adaptability Instruction: the Goal of Transition Programming," *Exceptional Children,* 1987, vol. 53, pp. 500-505.

Peterson, M., LeRoy, B., Field, S., and Wood, P., "Community-Referenced Learning in Inclusive Schools: Effective Curriculum for All Students," *Curriculum Considerations in Inclusive Schools: Facilitating Learning for All Students,* S. Stainback and W. Stainback, eds., Baltimore: Paul H. Brookes Publishing Co., 1992.

Sands, D., Adams, L., and Stout, D., "A State-wide Exploration of the Nature and Use of Curriculum in Special Education, *Exceptional Children,* 1995, vol. 62, pp. 68-83.

Stainback, S., Stainback, W., and Slavin, R., "Classroom Organization for Diversity among Students." *Educating All Students in the Mainstream of Regular Education,* S. Stainback, W. Stainback, and M. Forest, eds., Baltimore: Paul H. Brookes Publishing Co., 1989.

Stinson, D. M., Gast, D. L., Wolery, M., and Collins, B. C. "Acquisition of Nontargeted Information During Small-Group Instruction." *Exceptionality,* 1991, vol. 2, pp. 65-80.

Udvari-Solnar, A. and Thousand, J. S., "Promising Practices That Foster Inclusive Education," *Creating an Inclusive School,* R. A. Villa and J. S. Thousand, eds., Alexandria, VA: Association for Supervision and Curriculum Development, 1995.

Van Dyke, R., Stallings, M. A., and Colley, K. "How to Build an Inclusive School Community: A Success Story," *Phi Delta Kappan,* 1995, vol. 76, pp. 475-479.

Wehman, P. and Revell, Jr., W. G., "Transition from School to Adulthood: Looking Ahead," *Exceptional Individuals in School, Community, and Work,* W. Stainback, S. Stainback, and P. Wehman, eds., Austin, TX: Pro-ed, 1997.

Wiggins, S. B. and Behrmann, N. N., "Increasing Independence through Community Learning," *Teaching Exceptional Children,* 1989, vol. 21, pp. 20-24.

York, J., Doyle, M. B., and Kronberg, R., "A Curriculum Development Process for Inclusive Classrooms," *Focus on Exceptional Children,* 1992, vol. 25, pp. 1-16.